Dragons of the Deep

Origins & Lore

Dragons of the Deep

Origins & Lore

Dave Stone

MOON
BOOKS
London, UK
Washington, DC, USA

CollectiveInk

First published by Moon Books, 2026
Moon Books is an imprint of Collective Ink Ltd.,
Unit 11, Shepperton House, 89 Shepperton Road, London, N1 3DF
office@collectiveinkbooks.com
www.collectiveinkbooks.com
www.moon-books.net

For distributor details and how to order please visit the 'Ordering' section on our website.

ISBN: 978 1 917704 74 8
978 1 917704 73 1 (ebook)
Library of Congress Control Number: 2025937839

A CIP catalogue record for this book is available from the British Library.

Design: Lapiz Digital Services
Cover Artwork: The Tarot for the Sidhe. Dreamer 3 Card. Emily Carding. 2010. Schiffer.

UK: Printed and bound by CPI Group (UK) Ltd, Croydon, CR0 4YY
US: Printed and bound by Thomson-Shore, 7300 West Joy Road, Dexter, MI 48130

The manufacturer's authorised representative in the EU for product safety is:
eucomply OÜ - Pärnu mnt 139b-14, 11317 Tallinn, Estonia,
hello@ eucompliancepartner.com, www.eucompliancepartner.com

Contents

Introduction ix

Chapter 1: The Serpent from the Depths 1

Forged Within a Dragon's Thoughts 1

Symbol of War and Warlords 7

In the Wastes the Wild Dragons Roam 10

All That's Contained Within a Word 23

Serpents of Hearth & Home 28

Getting Cosmic 36

Dragon Slaying Saints 44

Chapter 2: The Oldest War 53

Chapter 3: The Benevolence of Dragons 70

The Dragon That Guards the Sacred Tree 70

Mothers of Dragons 92

The Immortal Healer 106

Chapter 4: The Alchemy of Dragons 112

The Serpent That Encircles the World 112

Orphism 117

Ophites 120

Agathodaimon 124

Abraxas 126

Chapter 5: What the Dragon Knows 127

Ningishzida – Prince of Dragons 129

The Grecian Caduceus 132

The Sceptre of the Dragon-King 134

Chapter 6: What Came First, the Serpent or the Egg? 138

Dissecting the Dragon 138

Endnotes 157

Bibliography 188

To the Old Serpent that girds
the earth like a belt and keeps
the content from spilling out into
the void. Thanks for that.

Introduction

To possess even a basic grasp of history is to embellish the world with another layer of understanding. Everything we see around us, from geological structures, to the advertisements on the local bus, are firmly rooted in the past. Everything has its history, it surrounds us in architecture, in place names, in events, in racial or ethnic diversities. As humans, we ride the cusp of the ever-onward-present, surfing the lip of the curling wave of Now. Our lives are lived amongst the ruins and remains of our ancestors. We are shadows who flit amongst the crumbling bones of history.

Still, it's certainly right to be wary; history can be revised, it can prove fickle and is open to the fashion of the times. To me, history is a series of windows through which we glimpse the past. Sometimes these windows are clearer than others, sometimes they need a good wipe. But history can give us a sense of place and a deeper understanding of forces which might appear beyond our control.

Twenty-plus years ago I began making a modest living carving stone. It's been a career that married my love of art with history. At the time, living in the city of Cork, I quickly exhausted the general Celtic studies sections in the library, moving on to the reference section, in which I discovered local archaeological tomes. In particularly I was drawn to artist renditions of objects found on digs. I scanned through book after book, copying these designs into sketchbooks, searching for images that I felt would look good carved on a stone. Over the past thirty years I've amassed a huge reference of motifs from libraries and sites in France, Scotland, England, Ireland, Wales, Greece, Italy and, nowadays, online.

It was only after I moved to Edinburgh and began a successful craft business that I began to realise I needed to know more about the designs – and not just collect the art! I needed to know their historical context and their significance. It was an ongoing concern, as I consumed tome after tome, delving into the myths and legends of Celt and Viking of the ancient world. It enabled me to talk about the different designs, their symbolism and meaning. We all want meaning, we hunger for it.

Dragons of Medieval European Art

Chapter 1

The Serpent from the Depths

Forged Within a Dragon's Thoughts

The shadow of the dragon permeates myth like the vital oil that lubricates the rough mechanics of legend. The imagery of this fierce creature dominates the covers of fantasy books and film posters. Modern TV series such as *Game of Thrones* and *House of the Dragon* have brought these magnificent beasts to life in all their awe-inspiring glory. Although our modern appreciation of the dragon is somewhat nuanced, in general, the dragon appears as a large, scaled creature, treading the earth with four powerful legs, each tipped by vicious claws. It can rise into the turbulent skies, born aloft on powerful wings, its long tail lashing behind it as it lets loose gouts of flame. The picture of shadowy dragons, pausing mid-flight to reign fiery destruction upon a helpless village, is still a terrifying motif. Yet, despite their proclivity toward chaos and death, there's also the image of the wise old drake, curling around its piles of glittering treasure. Here it is a creature that is venerable, ancient and wise.

Although the dragon graces the pages of many a fantasy, they have a history that runs parallel to our own. It is a long history, coiling and weaving through the snaky labyrinths of the past. From the lore of the Medieval era we are furnished with a plethora of dragon-like monsters: basilisks, chimeras, hydras and knuckers. These fabulous creatures haunt the faded pages of old bestiaries and were amongst the beasties that plagued the medieval mindset, populating the 'deserts' of the Christian hermits. And their lineage is older than this – for dragons are also glimpsed upon the ancient cylinder seals of the Sumerians as knotted serpents, hydra and beings that look suspiciously akin to the dragons we are familiar with.[1]

No matter which version of the dragon we come across, we can't help but admire them. Dragons inspire a sense of awe. Yet where does such imagery come from? Where are the precedents of the fierce and the wise beast? The quest for the answers to these will take us across the vast spread of continents: to China, India, and then back across the Aegean, and to Persia and ancient Mesopotamia – where a sky hero came to do battle with the Great Serpent itself. And then we will go further, deeper. We shall strive across much uncharted territory, coming face-to-face with the great dragons of old. Like alchemists in their laboratories, amongst racks of potions, unctions and copper urns labelled *solve et coagula,* we shall examine the myths surrounding them – uncovering that there is more to these legends than meets the eye. They are like the steady course of a river with many tributaries branching off – like the multi-headed Hydra that guards a golden fleece.

But before we pack our swords and set sail, perhaps we should ask ourselves why are we undertaking this quest? What motivates us? Our longing to hunt dragons? To slay them? Or is it something else? Could it be that there is some quality or qualities they possess that we admire? That we also wish to possess?

Dragons have always been magical beings. Whether they were frightening or benign, their blood, bones, teeth could all propagate fantastical effects. These are common themes that run like veins of precious metal through the mountains. The blood, teeth and even the eyes of dragons were sought after by sorcerers and wizards. It is no wonder that their symbolism was prized by Alchemists across Medieval Europe. The very nature of the dragon aligned them with the prime element of fire. Some were likened to living furnaces. This fiery breath is a much depicted feature of the dragon. But dragons were also creatures of water, air and earth and even encompass the fifth elemental realm of spirit too.

With such tremendous primary reactions powering the beast, it's no wonder that their bodies were believed to hold special powers. The writer, Pliny, was convinced that a precious stone was to be found inside the brains of dragons. It was called the *dracontia* or *dracantites* – though Philostratus reckoned that *dracontia* was actually the eye of the dragon. To own such an item was to possess the essence of the dragon itself – *dracontia* was the perfect jewel for any talisman.[2]

In the East we find a similar idea in the dragon pearl, which is sometimes shown in Chinese and Japanese art, clutched in a dragon's claws. Dragons coveted these pearls and stories tell of them seeking to reclaim stolen gems from foolish thieves. The pearl was viewed as the essence of the Moon: a sort of concentrated signature of the lunar orb, bestowed with its magical powers. In Japan these were known as *Tama* gems. Such ideas echo the alchemical nature of the dragon.[3]

The association with the Moon is interesting for, as well as its feminine and magical associations, the Moon controls the tides and affects the waters. One old story has it that the Moon is swallowed by a dragon at a lunar eclipse.[4] The mysterious race of beings known as, Nâga were known to possess magical stones, called *nâgamani.*[5] They glowed like miniature suns and they kept them in the back of their throats. This magical race was part-dragon and we shall meet them later on.

In the British isles, an object known as the Adder stone was used as a protective talisman. Accounts of what exactly this was vary in the folklore – ranging from hag-stones to fossils. However, an intriguing account is given by folklorist, J.F. Campbell. His journal references a Sutherland lady telling him of great white snake. The serpent never rested and a ring was formed by the slime from its own body. This ring sometimes fell off and, if found, brought luck and protected from disease. Campbell claims to have owned one and describes it as a glass bead of blue and white. This appears to be an ancient glass bead, and the description fits the Welsh, *Glain Neidr*. However, no matter how fanciful the nineteenth century folklorists may have been, their descriptions concur, and some form of midsummer ritual was associated with these stones. A Cornish tale reveals that to make adder stones a serpent must be struck in the middle with a hazel wand.[6]

Pliny describes the Adder Stone as being in the form of an egg. They were, he says, formed by numerous entwined snakes that gathered together in the summer. As they wriggled and slithered into balls they formed a substance called *anguinum*. Reporting to have heard this story from the mouths of Druids, Pliny describes the method by which these eggs were gathered: on a particular phase of the Moon, a Druid would wait near such a mass of serpents, cloak in hand. Once the egg was formed it would be "ejected by the hissing of the serpents" and the Druid would have to catch the ball in his cloak. It was imperative that the item shouldn't touch the ground. The Druid would then flee on horseback to evade the enraged snakes. Only by placing flowing water between them could their pursuit be halted. Pliny informs us that a genuine Druid Egg could float, and would try to make its way against the current. Some were fashioned into talismans, and were said to help their wearers in law-suits.[7]

Could these masses of serpents have been mating snakes? The stone an egg?

Eastern myths say that dragons lay eggs that took 3,000 years to hatch. In typical triadic form an egg required to spend 1000 years in water, another 1000 in the mountains and finally 1000 in the realm of humans. They are described as multi-hued gem stones that sweated moisture when it rained. The baby dragon would emerge in the form of a tiny worm, but could grow to full-sized in an instant.[8]

Another sought after substance was the blood which flowed through a dragon's veins. In one tale dragon's blood was used to restore a faerie princess who appeared from a rosemary bush – the king was besotted but she kept disappearing and the plant began to wither. The king's gardener overheard two dragons talking, and they unwittingly revealed that their blood could restore the rosemary to its former beauty, releasing the princess. Enlightened, the gardener slew the dragons and used their blood to revive the bush and reveal the princess.[9]

In the Norse tale of the *Volsungr Saga,* Sigurd slays the mighty dragon, Fafnir, at the behest of his foster father, Regin. The youth is then instructed to cook the dragon's heart and bring it to Regin, who desires its powers. But Sigurd burns his thumb while cooking the bloody morsel and sucks the blister. The scalding blood of the dragon brings the dragon-slayer the ability to understand the songs of the birds. It is from them that he learns of his foster father's treacherous nature.

But sometimes just tasting the blood of the dragon wasn't enough. In the *Nibelungenlied Saga,* Siegfried bathes in dragon's blood to gain superhuman strength and a skin which is as protective as a dragon's scales. However, as he bathes a linden leaf falls on his back, and here the blood fails to work its magic. This unprotected spot proves to be his Achilles heel.[10]

The Armenians had a myth that when the leader of Rome, Constantine, met with King Tiridates he presented him with a spear that'd been dipped in the blood of a dragon. King Arshak III also possessed a similar artefact whose blade could penetrate stone and caused infectious wounds that were beyond repair – however, he died at the age of 19.[11]

Being credited with the principle of moisture (the very essence of fertility and a necessary component for life), even a drop of dragon saliva was enough to make a young woman pregnant. Those who lay with a dragon would birth children who would subsequently forge powerful dynasties. Emperors in China often traced their lineage to their dragon ancestors.[12]

The teeth of the dragon could give rise to magical earth-born warriors, known as the *Spartoi,* or dragon-born. When Cadmus slew Ares' dragon at a sacred spring, he was gifted half of the teeth, as was Aeetes, the ruler in whose lands the Golden Fleece lay – itself guarded by another dragon. One Grecian writer even historicised the Cadmus myth, claiming that the *Drakon* was actually a person who Cadmus defeated in battle. The victor snatched tusks of ivory from his armour, keeping them as spoils of war (not dragon's teeth but boar tusks). These were stolen by Drakon's men and scattered across the countryside.[13]

In the Chinese tale of the *Sun and Moon Pool*, two *jiaolong* (a type of dragon) snatched the Moon and the Sun from the sky. Two human siblings set out to get the celestial bodies back. Hiding by their pool, they overheard the dragons speak of their terror of a golden axe that lay at the foot of a local mountain. Retrieving the item, the youths slew the *jiaolong* and then returned the Moon and Sun to their rightful places in the heavens. However, there was a problem, for the humans were tiny and the heavens so far away. So they ate the eyes of the dragons and grew in stature, until they were as tall as mountains. Using the trunks of tall trees they finally managed to return the celestial bodies to the skies. Pleased with their work, sister and brother remained by the pool, staring at the heavens. Two mountains next to the Sun-Moon Pool are named after them.[14]

In some cases, these properties and the dragons that they belonged to may well have been real phenomena. That large lizards were slain, and believed to be dragons paralleling those in mythology goes without saying. There are medieval accounts of such encounters. We also need to acknowledge that the occasional discovery of dinosaur bones and fossils must have also contributed to the law of the dragon. Such chance finds would have puzzled and perplexed those who came across them (and if you had to explain the huge femur of a plesiosaur, or the skull of a tyrannosaur then 'Dragon' was the likely 'go-to'). Such misconceptions were still prevalent even in the 19th Century. A dragon skull was displayed in the Hôtel du Ville, in Paris. The legend was that the beast had once inhabited a cave, until it was subdued by a valiant knight (who died in the endeavour). However, a Viennese professor recognised the skull as a fossilised rhinoceros' skull.[15] Its stone-like quality was a characteristic expected of dragon bones, hardened by the monster's internal fires. Indeed, dragon eggs were almost certainly types of stone and minerals. But to pursue such reductionist paths is to fail to grasp the origins of the dragon mythology and its lore.

The power accredited to the dragon was so great that even the picture of one could protect a person from harm. Talismans and imagery on items served a vital magical function, such as those from China which were worn as amulets for longevity. One story tells of a Chinese emperor who evaded an assassination plot because he was wearing his dragon clothes. Such a concept appears to be behind imagery that appears on ancient European armour and arms too.[16]

Symbol of War and Warlords

If the powers of the dragon were so famed and illustrious – that their mere image could somehow confer protection and courage, then it is no wonder their likeness was sought after by warlike man. From the earliest times the legendary power of the dragon was hungered for by warriors and leaders alike. By claiming the dragon as title, or as parent, men sought to use it as an allegorical symbol of war and martial might. Indeed, I have mentioned that the women who laid with dragons would give birth to sons of power (for the offspring of such a union was always male), and these leaders were emperors and progenitors of great dynasties. The mother of Alexander the Great was reputed to have laid with a serpent-dragon as part of a ritual – her dragon-born son went on to conquer much of the ancient world.

Across the globe, in China and Japan, people often used 'dragon' to refer to their leaders. Chinese emperors were born of them and its symbology surrounded them. They seated themselves upon the 'dragon throne', they slept in the 'dragon bed' and they were 'The True Dragon and Son of Heaven'. Even their clothes were embroidered with its imagery. The emperor was central to the stability of their empire. In this way they might offer themselves to be sacrificed should the rain not come – as Emperor Tang of the Shang Dynasty did (legend records that once his life had been taken rain did indeed begin to fall!) Fu-hsi, credited with being one of the founders of Chinese civilisation, was born in a dragon pool.[1]

A Grecian tale reveals that the people of Elis were brought a child from a mother who said she'd been imparted with prophecy during a dream. The child would fight for Elis. The soldiers took her babe and laid it before their forward ranks. As soon as the infant lay before them it became a snake and led the army to victory. Subsequently this snake-hero was worshipped under the name, *Zeus-Sosipolis*.

In 10th century Armenia, literary references are made to princes being like dragons; they were formidable, powerful and feared. In fact we still refer to people as being dragon-like or possessing the attitude of a dragon. But these phenomena weren't restricted to individuals, whole nations could trace their ancestry back to dragon lineage; such as the Slavs. The Bible references foreign peoples as dragons. The fiery Revelation is in fact a political text of agitation propaganda: the great dragon mentioned in the text is the Imperial Emperor of Rome, its many heads either a succession of tyrants or other hardline consuls. They were the 'then' enemy of the Hebrews… before that their dragons had been the Pharaohs. In this way a people are likened to the dragon in a negative sense. The Welsh united behind the red dragon, and its origins come from Celtic and Arthurian lore. Geoffrey of Monmouth tells of how Ambrosius (another name for Merlin) was to be sacrificed on the spot where king Vortigern wished to build a palace.[2] However, the youth told his captors that Vortigern's Druids had overlooked the fact that there was a sacred pool beneath that land. Doubting his words, the king had the ground dug up and, sure enough, their excavations revealed an underground pool. But this wasn't all, for two vases were discovered there, in which were two *würms*. This pair were locked in battle. One was red and the other white. Ambrosius said that the red would triumph and that it symbolised the Brythonic Welsh (Britons), while the white dragon represented the Angles – who would be vanquished. Still, it wasn't until the 1800s that the *draig goch* became the national symbol of Wales. King Arthur's father was Uther Pendragon – a name meaning Head-Dragon and denoting him as a warlord. Of the same period, the poet Taliesin often compares his hero, Urien of Rheged, to a dragon.[3] In these instances the dragon is invoked for its positive connotations as a power that epitomises strength and the authority to lead warriors into battle.

Just as men and nations abide under the martial spell of the dragon, so too its imagery covered military apparel. It appears on weapons and banners from early Zoroastrian times. Roman dragon banners, used in battle, were adopted by the Roman army after a defeat at the hands of the Parthians at Elegeia in 162 CE. These dramatic standards were made in a stocking style, so that they'd inflate with the wind, writhing as though they were alive. Scabbards and swords of the Celts feature much *dragonesque* imagery and are found spread over Europe, from Italy to Hungary. Some of these images may signify a semi-organised group of Celtic mercenaries; something that was recorded by Greek writers. It's well known that Celtic mercenaries were favoured by the Greeks and Macedonians.[4]

Cudgels were the most common weapon in early Mesopotamia. They were also the chosen weapons of the Vedic and Avestan gods. It shouldn't surprise us then that they were used by the dragon smiting Indo-Iranian mythic heroes. For this reason some were fashioned to resemble dragon heads.

Such ceremonial weapons were supposed to endow their user with the powers of dragons.[5] Thousands of years later the same intent is evident in England, where both the Tudors and Stuarts used the red dragon on their standards. The dragon appears on much medieval heraldry and the shock troops of the Middle-Ages were those first armed with the blunderbuss. This powerful gun was little more than a smaller version of a cannon, but portable. It discharged with such a roar that the men that used this weapon became known as *Dragoniers*.[6] Across Europe, warriors used images of dragons on shields, as banners or for embellishing their armour.

This phenomenon appears prolifically over the centuries. The use of the dragon in this context was intentional: to harness its fierce nature and to erode the will of their enemies in combat. This is a form of sympathetic magic, by which the imagery is believed to harness a desired essence or effect. The image is more than decoration, but magically projects outwards to cause fear, or it is believed to enhance the prowess of the warrior and even provide protection. So too, naming a warlord as a Dragon added a psychological edge to that individual's status and the way they were perceived by potential rivals.

In the Wastes the Wild Dragons Roam

From Ireland to Mesopotamia and beyond, dragons were consigned to wasteland and desert. The wilderness that plagued the early medieval mindset was filled with monsters. These were pagan places. Their dens were like suppurating sores, and in them the dragons waited.

It can't be denied that when humans began to farm, a certain dynamic must have taken place. Although the process was likely gradual, humans domesticated, not only their animals, but themselves. The patterns that governed hunter-gatherers were not the same as those necessary to survive a more agrarian existence. Settlement didn't equate to instant ease. The gains that skills such as husbandry brought were hard won. New patterns were needed. Patterns of thought, patterns in behaviour. But undeniably, humans had altered their world, and with it their world view. The longer people remained in the same location, the more bound to that land they became. With this came the need to identify with the land. And yet there existed a *separateness*; a sense of division between the raw world of the wilderness and that of civility – a division that would only increase with the passing ages. Even without the technological armour that affords our comfort, our ancestors must have begun to hold a distinction between *wild* and *domestic*. This distinction is common sense: you have a plot of land and grow crops, instantly the wilder side of nature is set against you. There are animals and birds that mess with the crop or munch the seeds before they've even had chance to sprout – not to mention insects: slugs, beetles, caterpillars that consume leaf and root. And then there are hidden forces: crop destroying bacteria, the health of nutrients in the soil – the lack of which could cause the crop to fail. And, on top of all this, the unhindered forces of Nature: storms and inundations could wreck everything. Certainly, the early farmers had a lot to fear of the wild.

With this in mind, perhaps we can understand that sense of fear many Neolithic people must have possessed for the wilder places. The places deemed deserts, wildernesses and wastes. The bleak heights of the mountains and the swampy marshes. Across Europe and beyond, these were the places less trampled, less tamed. It was such landscapes that enticed early Christian hermits to dwell alone, contemplating god – not exactly confronting themselves, for they projected their inner demons outward as manifestations of the world. A world that, to them, was inherently flawed and sinful.

However, even before the monks arrived on the scene, monsters had long penetrated the wastelands. And it should come as no surprise that these were the habitats favoured by dragons.

Perhaps this idea is reflected in the legend of Susa-no-wo, the Japanese storm god, who slew a dragon after he got it intoxicated on barrels of *saké*. The dragon had been terrorising the daughters of an earth god. After eating all but one, the dragon demanded the surviving daughter be surrendered to him in marriage. It was a huge beast, stretching over eight valleys. It had eight heads and eight tails and was covered in moss and trees. When Susa-no-wo finally slew it he hacked it to pieces, and the river turned red with its blood. Among its remains he found a powerful spirit sword.[1] In light of the animist ideas of Shinto, it is interesting that this dragon takes the form of the landscape itself. Susa-no-wo's fight could almost be interpreted as an assault upon the land, the imposition of order upon a perceived chaos.

Landlocked Armenia lies sandwiched between northern Turkey, Azerbaijan, Georgia and Iran. Humans have roved across its mountainous landscape for many thousands of years and there was much activity there in the Bronze Age. It forms something of a cultural crossroads, steeped in ancient history – and with this history comes the dragon. *Vishap* is the old Armenian word for dragon and appears to derive from one of the titles given to Azi-Dahaka: *Vishapa* (he whose spittle is poison[2]). It can also be used to refer to something 'great' or 'huge'. The name also references a series of megaliths found in the Armenian Highlands. These mysterious standing stones are dated to between 3000-2000 BCE. Many are fish-shaped and bear images of bull's heads. They are located in high mountains, at places associated with sacred springs and wells.[3]

The precipitous peaks and dizzying ravines of Mount Massis (known as Ararat by Europeans) have long been the abode of dragons, and their kind. This haunt has many old names. Among them is *Azat*, a name that means 'venerable'. Although the older mythology has been largely eclipsed by the medieval assertion that Noah's ark came to rest there, the slumbering volcano was also where a dragon and its witch-brood were once believed to dwell. This 'progeny of the dragon', the *Vishapazuns*, could change their forms between that of serpent and human. They were feared as magicians and versed in witchcraft.[4] Their great mother, Anush, dwelled in a deep ravine there.[5] In the time of King Artaxias (190 BCE), the leader of this tribe was named *Argavan*. He invited the aforementioned king to his palace on the mountain for a feast, intending to hatch a plot against Artaxias – but the plan was thwarted. Artaxias (helped by the fugitive Hannibal) is credited with reclaiming the kingdom of the Armenians from the Seleucids. His son, Artavasd, fared less well for it was said he'd been replaced with a changeling by the dragon-kind, and didn't live long. He was allegedly swept into the heights Mount Massis by dragons.[6]

Mountains hold a special place in people's imaginations. There's something mysterious and forlorn about the heights, they encompass great beauty and danger. In a tale that comes from Ukraine called, the Myth of the Glass Mountain,[7] a dragon takes up residence on a desolate hill in the kingdom of the Tsar. Fused into glass by the dragon's fiery breath, the mound swells as the beast feeds upon the people of the kingdom. Soon the dragon's perch is as tall as a mountain. Shiny and glassy, it's so huge that can be seen from anywhere in the kingdom, gleaming like a pyramid of quartz. The people, suffering beneath the dragon's rage, force the Tsar to petition warriors to help them. The Tsar complies, gathering the best warriors of the kingdom and these are dispatched to the Glass Mountain – but they don't last long. In fact they only succeeded in poking the hornet's nest, for the dragon descends upon the Tsar's castle itself. Ripping open a wall, it reaches inside and carries off his daughter, imprisoning her within its mountain.

It is a young prince named Ivan who finally beats the monster. He does this by listening to the advice of an ant, which tells him to bury a grain of wheat at the base of the mountain.

Ivan carries out this task. He plants the grain and it begins to grow, cracking the glass. In that same spot, fresh water begins to bubble. From spring to raging river the water flows, swelling from the deep and, as it does, the mountain melts like ice. The dragon, caught within the raging current, is carried off by the flood. Thus the lad earns the name 'Ivan the Dragon Killer.' He frees the princess and marries her.

This elemental tale hints at alchemical processes, as glass is created by a fusion of fire and silica. The melting mountain is reminiscent of the torrent that is withheld in the Vedic myth of Vrtra and Indra and that of Tiamat.[8] Of course, there's a moralistic element to this story too, because really it's the ant that defeats the dragon, and the tiny grain brings down the mountain: the smallest defeats the largest. It could be that this myth is also allegorical for the politics of the time, when people were oppressed by ruthless powers beyond their control.

The Danish settlers who colonised Iceland in the 10th Century AD, found a bleak and desolate land. A land that held immense beauty, but from whose ground the evidence of dragons was plain to see: the blackened earth, the smoking volcanoes, water that boiled and steamed despite the cold. It's no wonder that they reported they'd discovered a land in which dragons thrived. The milky waters of *Lagarfljót* (Lake Logurinn), to the east of the island, was home to one of these; a beast known as the *Lagar-fljótsomur*. But many other lakes and waterways on the island were said to have their resident drake too.

In the Norse myth of the *Volsung Saga,* young Sigurd was sent to combat the dragon, Fafnir. This dragon was once one of three brothers, and it was said that he'd murdered his father and stolen his treasure, taking it to his abode in the wilderness of *Gnitaheath*. It was there that he became a malevolent monster. However, these details were related to Sigurd by his treacherous foster-father, Regin – who desired the dragon's magical properties and its hoard for himself.[9]

This trope of wilderness and treasure is also evident in the Old English tale, *Beowulf*. In the last chapters of this ancient epic, Beowulf faces a terrible dragon in its lair within an ancient barrow. The lone mound sits upon the moors, close to the sea. Perched in such a remote location, this dragon's haunt appears to linger on a liminal frontier. The text relates that a straight path led there, but it was unknown to mortals. This reference enforces its location in an 'otherworldly' wasteland.[10] Beowulf, reveals a clear example of the dilemma that humans faced: the bitter-sweet relationship they had with the wild. Heorot is the great Danish hall, wherein sit the warriors – a place of feasting and merriment, of oath taking and where fealties are sworn. It is a beacon of light, warmth and human civilisation. Throughout the story, Heorot is contrasted with its malignant foes and the bleak wastes from which they come. The monsters range over the barren wastes, slinking into the hall to slay the sleeping warriors. The wicked Grendel, his mother and the dragon epitomise a fear of natural forces. It's also notable that Grendel's mother dwells in a cave that is located deep within a lake, its waters teaming with snakes and other reptilian beasts. To defeat her, Beowulf braves these deeps, and swims down to her cave. There are aspects to her that might remind us of another ancient Mother, Tiamat. But we shall deal with her in another chapter.

Other tales come from the mountainous regions bordering the Alps. In Switzerland a dragon was said to live inside a cave, upon which the Castle of Burgdorf stood. It was overcome by the heroic brothers Sintram and Baltram – but not before Baltram had been swallowed whole. Fortunately for him, his brother slew the dragon and opened up its belly to find Baltram still alive within. The lands around Mount Pilatus were also reputed to be inhabited by dragons, one of which dropped a dragon-stone that was retrieved by a peasant from Lucerne.[11]

The Tatzelwurm, or Stollenwurm, preferred to live in old mines and tunnels in the mountains. Although descriptions of them vary, they tend to stand on two feet and possessed a poisonous breath. Europe is alive with such monsters; they are woven into the fabric of the land. Like the dragons which infest the wilderness, these tales weave around bleak mountain fastnesses and infiltrate the darkest caves. Some dragons demand a yearly payment of a virgin girl as sacrifice, but are slain by intrepid heroes or saints and bishops. Churches are sometimes built upon the spot where such monsters fell. Versions of the dragon-slayer hero are especially popular, as are tales of three brothers who set out to rescue their younger sister from the clutches of a malicious horse-riding dragon.

The Christian mindset was especially honed to the sense that 'out there', in the wilds, beyond the relative civility of the monastery, demons roamed. Their world was populated with devils that sought to tempt the righteous from their chosen path. Every sin had its demons, but unlike the Hellenistic Greeks who saw their *Daimons* as something personal and beneficent, Christians saw them as external forces, hell-bent on evil. Dragons also ranged amongst the masses of these hellish legions.

However, we can't solely blame these evangelists and their converts for casting the dragon in this light. Although Christians were masters of appropriation, the dragon had been turned long ago... at least in the West. This dragon-slaying trope is much older than their creed, they merely took the existing symbolism, tweaking it to suit their needs.

Dragons enjoyed the solace of another type of abode: the deep, dark pool, pond or muir. In Aberdeenshire and Ayrshire the place-name, *Drakemyre* appears on the map – *myre* being a Scots word for boggy ground.[12] The dragon called the Knucker was reputed to prefer such watery holes too. This reptilian beast blew fire and spewed venom and is recounted in folklore from the South Downs of England. One such Knucker was said to snatch cattle and the occasional human too! It dwelled in the Knucker Hole at Lyminster, West Sussex – that was until a wandering knight slew it. Another version of the tale tells how a local, Jim Pulk (in some tellings *Puttock*), vied with the Knights who came to kill it. Instead of confronting it like they had, Jim baked a poison berry pie and left it next to the hole. Enticed by the smell of fresh baking, the Knucker arose from the waters and devoured the morsel. Overcome by the toxins it lay down to die and Jim snipped off its head with a scythe. A large stone, known as the Slayer's Slab,[13] is said to be Jim's tombstone. Although removed from its original location it's still displayed in the local church.

There are other 'knucker holes', and they are invariably filled with water. The waters of such pools are reputed to never freeze and were known for their curative properties.[14] The word, Knucker has its origins in the Anglo-Saxon word, *Nicor* – which describes a kind of hybrid sea monster.[15] The Old Icelandic *Nykr* is a fabulous water monster which equates with the old Germanic *Nixie*: a water nymph/sprite.[16]. Here we might catch a scent of something older, deeper... like gold coins glinting in peaty waters.

Sometimes the dragon emerges from its watery abode as a strange looking eel or worm. Such is the case in the 14th century story of the Lambton Worm.[17] This hideous beastie was discovered by a lord who preferred to go fishing on a Sunday than attend church. As if by divine punishment for his irreligious ways, he caught a nine-mouthed eel. Disgusted with his catch, he tossed it in a well (known as Worm's Well) where it grew in size while the lord was away on crusade. Returning to find that the dragon now ravaged the land, he made up his mind to destroy it. Taking the advice of a wise-woman, he had a special armour made for him – spear heads and daggers were fastened to his plate armour. Beast and man came together in the middle of the River Wear. The monster was a terror to behold, not only because it had grown in size, but its sulphurous breath was poisonous and its wounds regenerated quickly. Still, the lord's armour was the death of the monster, for as it coiled about him, the blades pierced its scales and it died. However, the old woman had warned the lord that he must kill the first living creature he came across once the worm was slain. He'd arranged to have his dog set free as he approached the castle, hoping it would come to him before he reached his castle. Unfortunately it didn't and the first living creature to chance upon him was his father. In despair the lord still slew his dog, but it wasn't enough to appease the old woman. A curse was set upon the lords of Lambton and for nine generations no lord died in his bed.[18]

A similar story appears in Scottish folklore and centres around St John's Town of Dalry, in Dumfries & Galloway.[19] In this tale the creature is described as a huge, white snake that grew so large its body curled around the old motte. For some time the locals tolerated the beastie, but one day, consumed by its vociferous appetite, the snake snatched up the body of a woman freshly interred in the kirkyard. It turned out that she'd been the wife of the local blacksmith, Michael Fleming. This incurred the blacksmith's wrath – not so much because he missed his wife, but rather he'd spent a fine penny on her burial. So he set to and made a suit of armour covered in sharp blades. When he went up against the snake, it simply eyed him slyly, opened its maw and gulped him down, swallowing him whole. Of course, soon the serpent realised its mistake as the blades opened it up from the inside, and Michael slid from within, along with the monster's entrails.[20]

There is actually a much older version that echoes both these legends. A Greek myth is told of a cruel dragon that lived at a spring at the foot of mount Helicon. Every year the dragon demanded a youth be brought to it to be devoured. One of its victims was Cleostratus, who wore a specially crafted breastplate upon which hooks were arrayed. As in the other tales, the beast gulped the warrior down, regardless of his armour. The barbed hooks forced the dragon to vomit the morsel back out, tearing the beast to pieces as the hero issued forth.[21]

For a land bereft of snakes, Ireland has its fair share of dragon stories. Some of them are quite mysterious, and the idea that the great serpent dragon begins life as a tiny worm is reflected in some of these tales too. For example, encompassed within the *Pursuit of Dairmuid and Grainne* is an unsettling story of a worm contained within a person: Cian mac Oilioll Olium was born with a caul on his head. It grew in size until he reached twenty years of age. He could never be shaved without slaying the man who attempted such a feat, presumably because they nicked his skin. But finally Scathan mac Scannlan armed himself for the task and slit open the caul with his knife. From the wound a worm slipped out, coiling around Cian's spear. Deciding not to kill it Cian departed (after his wound had been bound with healing herbs). The *Péist* was still knotted around his spear. Upon the advice of his parents the youth spared it, placing the worm in an enclosure. His mother cautioned that he and the serpent shared the same span of lifetime and its death might bring Cian's too. By the end of the first year the *Péist* had become an *ollphéist* with one-hundred heads. It was ravenous and ate everything they gave it, including warriors and heroes, armour and all. The fame of this marvel spread and a certain King of *Cairruidhe Luachra* went to see it, climbing upon the walls that encircled the beast. However, it pounced and struck the king, tearing off his leg. Horrified by this act Cian's father decided that the monster must be slain. His family surrounded the dun with wood and set it ablaze, hoping to burn the thing alive, but it shot into the air, and fled west, until it reached the cave of Fearna, in *Corca Ui Dhuibne*. The beast was eventually slain by one of the Fianna, Conan – however, we never learn if Cian also died.[22]

The worm also makes an appearance in minute but magical form, usually imbibed alongside a drink and giving rise to miraculous births. Cu Chulainn is conceived this way and emerges from his mother's womb clutching a worm in each hand.[23] The imagery is as fascinating as it is repulsive, and is reminiscent of some Celtic carvings.

Dian Cecht, the Healer of the godly Tuatha De Danaan, discovered three serpents coiled within the heart of Mechi, a son of the Morrígan. His aspect was terrible to behold and the gods slew him, foreseeing that he'd bring nothing but trouble. These serpents would have grown to destroy Ireland, so the tale relates. Dian Cecht tossed them into the waters of a river which boiled as the snakes drowned. The River Barrow derives its name from proto-Celtic, **boru-* to 'boil', 'brew'.[24]

As for the Conan who slew the *ollphéist,* another myth is told of his dragon-slaying exploits. Like all good stories, it has a few versions. One is that Conan carelessly tossed a worm into a lough and it swelled in size. This serpent was known as the Caoranach. It laid waste to the land. In uproar, the people turned to Conan, blaming him for their grief. Thus the hero, dagger in hand, strode to the rise of Knochnacunny, where the Caoranach's food was delivered, allowing the monster to swallow him whole. As he was gulped down into its entails, he got to work slicing through the side of the Caoranach. The effect of the juices in the beast's entrails cost Conan his hair and he was known from that day on as Conan Maol (bald). The lough, which was known as the Fair Lough at the time (*Finlough*) filled with so much blood it was hence-forth known as Lough Derg (Red Lough). Legend has it that the remains of the Caoranach's body metamorphosed into great stones, and that upon one of these the image of the monster was fashioned.[25]

Another version has it that the heroes of the Fianna battled a two-fingered witch and her giant son. Ambushing them in Munster, the witch's son slung his ma over his shoulder and fled. However, as he lumbered across the land, he was unaware that she'd been slain by a sliver-tipped arrow. By the time he reached Finlough, much of her body was gone; smashed to bits upon the landscape. Later, the Fianna came across her remains, but were warned by a dwarf that they should leave the thigh bone alone, for it contained a worm. Conan Maol cracked the bone and took the worm on the tip of his spear, lobbing it in the lough and shouting after it: "Here's enough water for you." Instantly the worm grew into a terrifying monster and began ransacking the land. The leader of the Fianna, Fionn mac Cumhail, learned that the serpent had a weak spot: a mole on its left side. Using this knowledge to his advantage, he attacked and crippled the beast, enough that it hid within the Loch.[26] According to this version, it was Saint Patrick who later arrived in the area and finished the job with his crozier.

There are forty-two islands in Lough Derg (often cited as a bleak place by visitors past and present). One of these is called Saint's Island (also recorded as *St. Dabheogs*), upon which are the remains of an old convent of Canons Regular of the order of St. Augustine, where pilgrims were catered for. The complex was in use until the 16th Century AD, when it was destroyed by Protestant settlers. An old fable had it that a tunnel connected Saint's island to Station island – where the gateway to Purgatory lay, known to this day as Patrick's Purgatory.[27] However, since this tunnel couldn't be found, pilgrims were conveyed by coracle to Station Island. The 'Stone of the Caoranach' was described in the 1700s by Richardson as being a large flat rock, upon which the image of a wolf-like beast was carved, with a serpent tail between its legs and slung over its back. The stone had been discovered by Ludovicus Pyrrhus, in his failed attempt to locate the gateway to Purgatory. It appears that this was an old medieval carving from the ruined convent. Daniel O'Connor describes it in the late 1800s. St Patrick's Purgatory was located nearby, as were the petrified bones of the Caoranach, which ranged along the shore of the remotest point of the island – the most distinctive part of this natural feature earned the name *leac na mbonn* (Flat Stone of the Feet) and was described as smooth and flat, with a circular depression at its centre. The rock was reported to have curative powers for the feet of road-weary pilgrims.

In the 1400's an Italian, Antonio Giovanni de Mannini, recorded his pilgrimage to St Patrick's Purgatory. There he was told about a demon called Corna, which was described as an evil bird – this might well be a corruption of the old Caoranach myth.[28] However, the word is likely a misspelling of Corra (*corr/corra,* Gaelic for stork: *corra-glas* is heron, *corra-ghrian,* bittern) – The bird in question appears to reference the heron, a bird that was revered by the Druids. However, to confuse issues further, another Corra features in the legends associated with St. Patrick. Modern references also refer to a mountain goddess, said to reside on Croagh Patrick before the Saint chased her to Lough Derg.[29] In this Christian narrative the monster is female and she's the mother of the devil. She's also named as Caoranach (spelt *Caorthannach*) in a version where the saint pursues the beast down the mountain, through Lough Nacorra and down to Lough Derg, where he finished her off.[30] The Caoranach was also known as Caol.

Here we see the enduring nature of the dragon myth. Even if it is has become confused with the passing of time, as if seen through a misty veil, the essence remains.

Amongst the many stories that have gathered about Fionn Mac Cumhail, there is mention of a 'cleansing' that takes place as the Fianna work their way around the wildernesses of Ireland slaying giants, spectres and other foul creatures. Unfortunately, the list is incomplete and the story's climax remains lost, but of the thirty monsters named, seventeen are serpents and four are monsters or reptiles. The intriguing thing about this list is that the majority of the serpent-dragons dwell in loughs, rivers or wells. This association with watery domains is persistent and widespread. By association water is an extension of these 'wilds'. Watery depths were unfathomable to most humans, especially in the past when luxuries such as diving equipment didn't exist. This watery theme is one that we will examine much closer in subsequent chapters.

All That's Contained Within a Word

The Gundestrup cauldron was created in the 1st century CE. The artefact was likely commissioned by a Celtic warlord or Druid. Wrought by Thracian silversmiths, it depicts scenes of Celtic deities. This mysterious artefact was found in a Danish bog, and had been carefully dismantled before being placed as an offering by a deep, dark pool. On one panel a bearded figure stares out as he grips two dragons by their necks. Such a character might put us in mind of the Celtic dragon-slayer Fionn mac Cumhail. The dragons are very detailed, they have wings and forearms and wouldn't be out of place in a medieval manuscript from a thousand years later.

Dragons vary in form, they might be gigantic, four-legged with an array of snarling heads, or appear as giant serpents. Medieval bestiaries are filled with images of monsters and dragons. Their authors took many mythic creatures from Classical mythology, adapting them within a Christian framework: in which they were associated with the Devil and epitomised sin. They left us with some beautiful imagery. A number of dragon types are named. There was the Wyvern – portrayed as winged and supported upon two legs that resemble those of an eagle. Its tail is often barbed with a cruel and poisonous spike. The Chimera is a hybrid creature, formed of the body of a goat, the tail of a dragon, with the head and mane of a lion. It was reported to be agile and strong, breathing fire as it flew over ancient Lycia. Hesiod reckoned it to have three heads: lion, goat and dragon. The hero Bellerophon downed it with arrows as he pursued it on the winged horse, Pegasus. In Lycia, at Olympos, you can still visit the site where it plunged to the earth and where flames jet from the ground.[1] The Hydra had a dog-like body and nine snaky heads, although other accounts credit it with many as 10,000, while the Cockatrice is the result of a hen's egg hatched by a serpent. Its head is like a cock, replete with ruddy comb, while it retains the wyvern's body. Its breath is deadly poison and its staring gaze brought death. Like the Wyvern, its tail was tipped by a poisonous sting and it was winged. The Hermetic god, Abraxas was of this ilk.[2] The Amphisbæna, or Amphista was a dragon whose tail terminated in a serpent's head (it was sometimes portrayed on old crosses of the Dark Age period in Britain, and also appears on Pictish stones). The king of the serpents was the Basilisk, so called for his crest. Pliny mentions them as being the terror of other monsters, which flee from it. To catch its eye meant certain death, and its breath was a poisonous cloud. Such was the power of its death-dealing eye, and if a Basilisk were to catch a glimpse of itself in a mirror it would frighten itself to death.

Way to the East, far away from the scribes of Europe, the Chinese dragon bore a long and venerable legacy. Dragons appear in much Eastern art, and there were very precise ideas of how they should appear. It was written that a dragon was composed from nine resemblances and three joints. The three joints were divisions from head to shoulder, shoulder to breast and breast to tail. The nine resemblances were the horns of a deer, the head of a camel, the eyes of a devil, the neck of a snake, the abdomen of a clam, the scales of a carp, the claws of an eagle, the paws of a tiger and the ears of a cow. If the dragon possessed a lump upon its head (*chi mu*[3]) it could ascend to the sky. Those without were earthbound. The standard oriental dragon has whiskers on either side of its mouth. Its horns are usually sturdy spikes rising from the back of the head. It is regarded more fish-like than amphibian-like, hence references to carp scales. There are similarities in their depictions in oriental art to koi carp[4] (if you ever observe this magnificent fish gracefully rising from the depths of a pool the association is understandable).

Across every land, it seems dragons once roamed. Their origins are deep and stretch back to the dawn of history. Some possibly existed, others were symbolic. Men could become them. Women could sleep with them. Throughout the ages dragons have been with us and in that time they've gathered much in the way of symbolism, like the scales pinned to their hides. The dragon, as a symbol, has permeated human civilisation. There's hardly a place in the world that the idea of it hasn't touched. Its imagery spans gulfs of time within our collective and personal unconscious minds. Numerous theories and rational explanations have been given by writers for their existence. While some of these may be true, or truths attached to the phenomenon that is 'dragon', they are only ever facets.

We can see that there are various ways of depicting the dragon, yet a distinction must be drawn between the image and its symbolism. The image is the way a thing looks, its appearance to us. A symbol is what it means. Its deeper implications. Dragons across the world consist of these two elements, and we should explore them both. There's also a distinction to be made between dragons of mythology and dragons from folklore. Those of myth and legends are usually celestial beings or beings of elemental nature, sometimes associated with sovereign or divine power. They form the oldest strata of legend. The folkloric versions tend to be later, and are more immediate. Such tales are firmly rooted amongst the people of rural communities. In its folkloric form the dragon is often seen as mischievous, malignant or something to be overcome. Mythic Dragons in the East are beneficiaries, associated with great fortune, while those in the West were portrayed as dangerous harbingers of chaos. However, this being said, we shall begin to see that this wasn't always the case. Evidence suggests that, at one time, even in the West the dragon was something all-encompassing, all-powerful.

References to Great Serpent and the use of Dragon inevitably entwine. To a large degree they are inseparable. This is somewhat reflected in the various names given to these creatures. They are like shadowy trees in the mists of time – great oaks in whose trunks a lineage is maintained and in whose branches history unfolds. Their names once conjured fear, awe and great respect. But like a hero, tip-toeing into the dragon's lair, we should tread lightly here. Just because a creature is described as '*a dragon*' doesn't mean it was. Sometimes translators used the wrong words, or found an 'umbrella word' where no others sufficed. But names are important, for like the dragons, they have a lineage, and a point.

In the language of the Norse, they were both *Dreki* and *ormr*. The first comes from the Latin, *Draco*, itself deriving from the Greek, *Drakōn*. Although this is a 'loan word' it doesn't mean that dragon myths were brought to Scandinavia at this date. *Ormr* is their original name and predates *Dreki*[5] (the Norse word *Naðr* means snake, pointing to a recognised difference between the two). The Old English 'Drake' comes from the Saxon, *Draca*. While the name *wyvern* is derived from the Saxon word *wivire*, which means serpent. This creature has a coiling trunk and bears a pair of eagle's legs tucked beneath its wings. There is also the legless and wingless *guerive*, which would seem to be a serpent, but a powerful one, with a dragon's head, horned and bearded. *Lindworm* itself comes from *Linnormr*,[6] a mythical snake-dragon with the prefix, *linn* meaning 'torrent/waterfall'. We can see here that *ormr* becomes *würm* (*wyrm/worme*), which can mean both serpent or grub.

Although the disappearance of the serpent (*naithair* in Irish) from Ireland's shores is ascribed to Saint Patrick, there exists a body of law that references the *ollphéist* (pronounced *oll-feysht*). *Oll* is a prefix meaning huge and *Péist* (with a h inserted when the prefix is before it) can mean a 'fabulous beast', a monster but also a worm. This mirrors the Irish name of the dragon: *piast* or *péist* which means pest or beast, but along with terms such as *uile-bheist* refers to the lough dwelling dragon. In Scots Gaelic it is *Beithir-nimh*: a poisonous serpent that lives in the rivers.[7] References to eels also occur in Irish mythology: the goddess Morrígan shifts into this form when she fights the hero Cú Chulainn at the ford. Bearing in mind that the Anglo-Saxons use the word *würm* in reference to dragons and given the watery locations of many *ollphéist,* I believe we're talking about the same thing. The historical links between the islands of Ireland and Scotland were established thousands of years ago. Further strengthening this watery link are place names found, mostly in Co. Clare and around the limestone wilderness of the Burren. These include Poulnapeasta (Pool/hole of the *Péist*).[8]

Latin *Serpens* is the winding creature, *coluber,* the coiling animal. There was a *Coluber* that was described as a serpent-dragon, which inhabited the River Dordogne and often attacked voyagers. It was reputed to actually dwell in a cave in the Couze Valley, until it was destroyed by a local bishop. One particular *Coluber* was associated with a spot where an underground river exits at the Valcluse Fountain, until it was forced to flee to the Alps by another saint (Véran).[9]

But perhaps the most revealing of these ancient names is that of one of the mythological dragons of old: *Ophis,* whose name means 'the seeing one', or 'one that sees around'. In fact Greek, *Drakōn* translates as 'one that looks into a thing or person' – deriving from *Derkomai,* 'to see with clarity'.

The Image from the Gundestrup Cauldron

Serpents of Hearth & Home

So we see that dragons and serpents are interchangeable and often indistinguishable. This isn't surprising, for what unites them are their mythological parallels. As we shall see (and are perhaps already beginning to suspect) these similarities unite them in a very deep strata of ancient belief.

Snakes hold a fascination that puts many of us in awe, while others, driven by innate instincts of self-preservation, flee. The rippling fluidity of their movements, the way they glide across the ground, or the way they can suddenly turn, rearing to dart and jab – even the texture of their skin possesses a hypnotic quality. Although natural observations can lead to many analogies, and have been used in attempts to fully explain dragon myths, they can never truly explain the huge body of lore attached to them. Still, we have to recognise that visually, the way a serpent moves, their size, their potentially lethal bite and their similarity to branches or roots, must have borne some influence. Yet, given the scope and the profusion of these myths and fables we must ask ourselves, *why the snake?* Arachnids are equally as terrifying, fascinating and dangerous. Why don't they fill the myths and legends to the same extent? Why aren't there *cosmic spiders* and heroic spider-slayers? Serpents and their mythic cousins have gripped the human psyche.

Snake imagery permeates ancient culture precisely because they, and the symbolism attached to them, were all important. It might be that the spirals carved on some of the oldest human monuments and standing stones of the Megalithic period are representations of serpents. But this imagery is more than just 'snake'. More than scale and flesh and bone. As a personification of energy the serpent also represented great mystery and related to cosmic forces. In Egyptian mythology snakes played a somewhat demonic role, but they could be harnessed for beneficial purposes. Egyptian texts reiterated that these creatures be treated with respect, for they were the primal beings and related to the primordial serpent, Sito. It was even told that the High God's tears gave rise to the brood of serpents.[1] They were the oldest of the old, and it was best to tread with care around them.

An informative myth from *The Book of the Heavenly Cow*, relates how their powers were suppressed: The high god Atum set a seal upon them, forbidding the snake to cause harm. However, Mankind rebelled against the gods, and Atum departed, leaving the seal ineffective and the serpents' true nature was revealed. In response Atum addressed the God Geb to instruct the serpents that their place was within the earth and their powers, which are great, were to be used for the good of the world, not against it.[2] The snakes were blessed with a magical power in their mouths, they knew great spells, and they were blessed of *Hikê*.[3] Although Atum could no longer ward over them as he once did, his son, Osiris assumed this role as one of his godly functions.

Given such lofty ideals associated with the snake, it was good measure to keep one about the house. The household snake was a symbol of prosperity and fortune, and offerings were left for them. The custom is known in India (*Vasta-Sarpa*), in Latvia, Bosnia-Herzegovina and Lithuania. Sometimes they were buried beneath the threshold, as recorded in Sweden. In ancient Minoan culture the goddess of the household became associated with snakes. Cappadocian Greeks had the *sifótēs*, while Armenian *Sahapet* were spirits of the household that took the form of serpents. In other parts of the country they were named *Dovlat* or *Barak'at* (wealth and welfare), and *Tnapan*, 'the protector of the house'. Carving them on lintels and doorways served the same purpose. In ancient Illyria and they were called *žaltys* or *gyvate*.[4]

Dwelling in holes perhaps linked snakes to the Underworld. They appear on hundreds of funerary vases in Greece, and their images are carved on the sides of many sarcophagi. Plutarch says that Greeks even visualised their heroes as serpents.[5] Cecrops is the most ancient of the Athenian heroes. The mytho-historical version has it that he arrived there from Egypt, with a small group of settlers in 1556 BCE. In the Attic lands he found the locals living in remote settlements, divided and struggling to survive. Cecrops galvanised these people and formed a community, giving laws and teaching them to cultivate the olive. This newfound settlement was the beginnings of Athens. However, this historical account fails to mention that Cecrops was half-serpent. His serpentine tail has been explained as representing his instigation of marriage between one woman and one man. Though this explanation seems to lack substance we shall see that it perhaps hints at a profounder aspect of this serpentine worship.[6] In ways this half-serpent ancestor who lays down law and promotes civilisation reflects Berossus' accounts of Oannes, the half-fish man, and the exotic Quetzalcoatl.[7]

The second Athenian ancestor is a bit of an enigma, as he is often depicted as a large, bearded serpent. Erichthonios was originally a fertility deity of the fields, but became the ancestral founder of Athens. He is the child of the failed sexual encounter between Hephaistos and Athena. One version of this interaction was that the over-excited smith god ejaculated prematurely and drips of his semen splashed against Athena's leg. In disgust she wiped off the mess with a piece of wool and tossed the rag to the ground. From this soil Erichthonios arose. He is Earth-born, hence the snake symbolism that accompanies him.[8] Athena rejected the babe and gave him to Gaia, the Earth Goddess, who raised Erichthonios until he became a boy and then returned him to Athena. His mother then placed him in a sealed basket and passed him into the care of Cecrops and his three daughters, forbidding them to look upon the child. Despite the warning curiosity overcame them. The three girls opened the lid to peer within. Inside they beheld a child encircled by a serpent. In other depictions the youth is portrayed as half-serpent, or as a snake. One image, from an Amphora in the British Museum, depicts Erichthonios sitting in an open basket with two serpents either side of him. One of these is bearded male, the other is feminine (it's worth noting here that in Egyptian imagery the bearded snake is always male).[9] This has been interpreted by some scholars as symbolising the rejuvenation of the old Serpent King – a ritual rebirth[10] – but, as with Cecrops, the inclusion of masculine and feminine serpents is not without reason and something we shall cover in a later chapter.

When the ancient historian, Pausanias visited the Parthenon in its heyday, he stood before the great statue of Athena and described that by her feet lay a huge shield and a snake. This symbolised Erichthonios.[11] Descendants of his lineage wore a golden serpent. In this sense the snake may represent masculine characteristics, those of a phallic nature. Erichthonios is associated with the fertility rites of *Arretophoria* and *Themophoria,* which included the carrying of small baskets of bread. These sacred loaves were fashioned into images of humans and snakes. This ceremony involved the carrying of dew-laden boughs by the *Hersephoroi*, the drops of which were seen as sacred and life-bearing.[12]

Amongst the Greeks it wasn't only their kings who were of serpent origin. Diodorus Siculus wrote of the Scythians that, before they were named, a half-serpent woman was born amongst them from the earth. She lay with Zeus and had a son called Scythes, from whom the Scythians came. It's as though a vestige of an earlier belief is hinted at here. The sky god named by the Grecian author is Zeus, but it is more likely that the Scythians had their own sky god, who lay with their earth goddess.[13]

Hopefully the status of the snake has been somewhat elevated in your eyes. Even as the humble household guardian, we glimpse a sense of its power. The phenomena could be likened to a subdued ripple working outwards from a central point. But we want to voyage onward, driving toward the central point... to the creature that disturbs the waters and creates these ripples. The closer we get, the larger these ripples become. So, let's now sail toward those larger ripples. Here the serpent remains, but it gathers force and momentum. Here we find a sacred creature, an echo of something more divine. For, in tandem to their symbolism, we find the cults dedicated to the serpent winding their way across the Eurasian subcontinent and Europe long before they harried the toes of Christian monks.

From ancient Sumerian cities clay tablets of the 3rd millennia BCE make reference to snake-walkers and serpent-charmers, hinting at the antiquity of human fascination with these species. But this was more than just the longing to hold and be close to them. These were professions that served sacred functions, and weren't acting solely on personal whims. Their snake-charming involved sacred chants, something that wouldn't have been amiss in the temples of Hindu deities or the ceremonies of the Egyptians. In the village of Shinrala, India, Shiva worshipping serpent-handlers were taught from youth how to hold poisonous cobras. They learned to stifle their inner fears, and instead view the snake with love and affection – qualities they believed would avert its deadly bite.[14] This ambivalent attitude towards serpents is also found in Grecian Dionysian worship.

Perhaps we can get a taste for the divine nature of the snake from an Egyptian legend of primeval Sito. It was written that this being arose from the cosmic waters as the first manifestation of the high god. Sito personified the first divine word, the word that spoke itself into being. It was named 'Provider of Attributes', *Neheb-Kau*. It was the primal guise of *Atum*. The High God and this Serpent were the same and yet they were also separate – as though the delineation of creation was the result of some cosmic contradiction: Atum was both the Serpent and yet the god existed independently within its coils. Sito was the first pulse of energy and the scribe of the divine book that recorded what has been and effects what's to come. *The Book of the Dead* reveals that at the end of time, when all is reclaimed by the infinite potential of the primordial void, Atum will once again assume serpent form.[15]

This heady cosmological concept, idealised in the form of a gigantic serpent, is powerful imagery. Yet, on a less lofty scale, the mystery of the serpent prevailed. Just as the macrocosm reflects the microcosm, the *genus loci*, or spirit, of sacred places was viewed as snake-like.[16] These were particularly prevalent at springs and wells.[17] Thus it was only natural that this association between symbol and image was carried into temple worship. Many kept snakes within their precincts.

In ancient Greece, there once existed a centre of the cult of Asclepius the healer. Known as *Asclepions*, they were sanctuaries where those suffering from illness would undergo a series of rituals: including sleeping overnight in a sacred precinct; awaiting healing dreams from the god himself. Three-hundred *Asclepions* have been identified within the ancient world of the Hellenes, with the most famous located at Epidaurus. Snakes were the sacred animal of these temples. The healing undertaken there was achieved in a regulated fashion: patients would spend some time in a dark room, where they rested (incubation) and hoped to receive the god. During this time other rituals were undertaken, including the touching of the area that was blighted with a serpent or wand. Therapies for each patient were meticulously planned and also included surgeries, medicines, diets, exercise and recuperation, with the patient attending ceremonies and receiving spiritual care.[18] It should also be noted that Asclepius had a daughter named Hygiea, famed for her powers of healing. She's portrayed as a young woman, around whose arm a serpent twines, with its head resting upon a shallow dish.[19] From this goddess we get the word hygiene.

The god Asclepius sometimes assumed the form of a great serpent[20] – an act which is represented in ancient imagery. He was said to have been trained in the use of healing herbs by the wise centaur, Chiron, who dwelled on Mount Pelion. The rod of Asclepius is a symbol that is still known to this day. It consists of a staff with a serpent winding along its length. Eusebius of Caesarea explains the serpent's use was because it was the creature most full of spirit (*pneuma*). It had discovered the remedy for clear sight and knew the whereabouts of the plant that restored life[21] (we might recall here the origins of the word, *Drakōn* and *Ophis*). In another story Asclepius was brought this plant by a serpent. Allegedly St Hilarion, an evangelising Christian, slew a giant Boa at Epidaurus. This was a highly significant act, and probably a death knell for the healing cult.[22]

The power of serpent as oracle can be witnessed in the Grecian cult of Glycon, which the writer Lucian describes in some detail. He viewed it as a hoax and scandal. The cult was founded by a self-styled prophet, Alexander the Paphlagonian, and centred around a huge python, garbed with a human mask, and claimed to be an incarnation of Asclepius. Despite Lucian's dislike of the cult, it flourished in the 2nd Century CE and persisted into the 3rd.[23] It was only one of many such groups, some of which have their origins in the mystery cult of Orpheus.

The sect known as the Naassenes, a gnostic sect we shall look at later, were documented by a cynical scholar named Hippolytus. His observations are interesting, as he suggests that they believed that everything, all matter, and all spirit were formed of serpents. And it is to be noted that the famed Armenian saint, Gregory, wrote that all will learn the wisdom of the serpent.[24] Ancient Armenian archaeology has found images of a divine serpent whose body separates the heavens and the earth (dated from 600-700 BCE). Belief of a world-girding serpent seems to have featured in ancient religions of that region. The cycles of the Sun and Moon were explained by the actions of this cosmic serpent, swallowing and spitting them back out. Imagery of this belief is still present in carvings from the 10th CE in Georgia.[25]

In the mystery religions of Greece, philosophers speculated about the form of spirit, or *pneuma*. Hundreds of years later, Clement of Alexandria, a fervent Christian, said the soul was snake-like. Another Christian, Porphyrius, Bishop of Gaza, also believed that *pneuma* exited the dead in serpent form.[26] This belief was extremely ancient and worlds away from that of doctrinal Christian thought. In ancient Greece, not only was the serpent seen as the bearer of the dead, *it was the dead*. This association is evidenced by the profusion of serpent imagery that accompanies funerary monuments from across the sphere of Grecian influence.

This concept was rationalised by Plutarch, who tells a story about an event in Alexandria: when Ptolemy disgraced the body of the Spartan king, Cleomenes, he had the body hung up and impaled. Not long afterwards, guards witnessed a huge snake winding around the corpse's head. Crowds gathered to salute Cleomenes as a hero. However, several learned men arrived on the scene to dispel the ignorance of the people. They explained that, just as corpse of animals gives life to beetles, so too the juices of the human corpse congealed to form serpents.[27] Whatever the 'facts', people associated the serpent as a symbol of both hero and the dead.

The serpent features in so many cultures across the globe in vital and surprising ways. We've inherited an anti-serpent bias, partly through the appropriation of the serpent via Christianity as 'the deceiver', the slimy sly snake that appeared in the Garden of Eden and tempted primal man and woman with self-consciousness. Despite the power of the metaphor, it's unfortunate that the serpent became associated in this way with evil and therefore, by default, Satan. Much Christian myth alludes to serpents and serpentine demonic powers in a negative light. The snake was vilified and became a scapegoat for the shadow side of human-nature.

Even the famed Islamic shrine, the *Ka'ba,* was built upon a serpent – which tradition described as a two-headed wind that wound about the holy shrine. However, it was viewed as divine and not demonic. Another tale tells that Mohammed himself set a white serpent with the head of a goat to watch over the *Ka'ba*'s treasures. Serpent monsters were not uncommon as guardians of offering shrines in pre-Islamic times, and the 'horned' serpent appears in Celtic lore too.[28]

Getting Cosmic

Although they are the object of many a scary story, dragons were also celebrated. One English Folk custom involved carrying a dragon in a bawdy, but light-hearted parade. This procession marked the Battle of Burford that was fought in 752 CE, in which Cuthred of Wessex won a victory over Æthelbald of Mercia. A standard bearing the image of a golden dragon was allegedly taken from the loser. The celebration was forgotten in the early 20th century but it was resurrected again in the 1970s.[1]

In Metz, a procession to honour the dragon-slaying Saint Clement, paraded an effigy of their local dragon, *Graolly*, through the town. In Tarascon it was the image of *Tarasque* that was carried through the streets of the town by a girl who represented Saint Martha. The procession celebrated a legend in which Martha saved the town from a terrible dragon that rose from the Rhône. The Tarasque was described as having a huge carapace, like a tortoise shell, which was covered with sharp spikes. The saint subdued the monster by splashing it with holy water. The parade is still held to this day and to touch its image brings fortune. A similar account of a dragon-parade is given from Mons, in Belgium, and to pluck a streamer from the dragon-effigy's hide supposedly bestows luck. This dragon is driven through the town where it is slain by an actor playing the role of either St. George or Gilles de Chin, a local hero.[2]

Such examples are celebrations of the defeat of dragons, themselves being extensions of the Christian zest for slaying them – which in turn may well be an extension of earlier religious schism. For example, a festival called *Mihragān* celebrated the vanquishing of the Great Dragon, *Ahi Dahaka* and occurred around the Autumnal equinox. It appears that the festival was a time to praise the forces of good and brace for the coming winter. The celebration was maintained until the arrival of the Mongol hordes and has seen a revival in the modern Zoroastrian faith.[3]

Not all Western dragons were evil and sometimes even the most ravenous of beasts might be tamed by the kind words of a maiden – as in the Armenian myth of Odz-Manouk. This royal child was born as a snake, but quickly grew in size and became a dragon. Discovering the dragon's penchant for female flesh, a daily quota of maidens were rounded up across the kingdom to satisfy the monster. One day, the guards were surprised to see that one female victim was still alive. The girl, Avevhat, talked to the dragon kindly and not been frightened by his appearance.[4]

The ancient Slavs were formed of various ethnic groups of eastern Europeans and migrating tribes, such as the Huns. The Scythians and Alans had already been amalgamated into their tribes. During what is known as the Migratory Period, which lasted from around 300-600 CE, the Huns pushed west, filling the void left by Germanic tribes – who migrated west and south in reaction. Thus the cultural heritage of the Slavic people forms a bridge that incorporates imagery from both east and west. Eastern influence is evident in their art and stories – and this shouldn't surprise us, considering contact between China and the Slavs' Scythian ancestors. Thus, Slavic *zmaj* were protective dragons. They fought against atmospheric demons that brought on crop-destroying hail. Descriptions vary, but they were hybrids of human and dragon, while other accounts describe them as fiery birds who unleashed showers of sparks as they flew about their business. They were known to breathe either red or blue flames.[5] There was also Simorg, a fierce dragon of folklore who was also a personal spirit dragon, protecting family and home.[6]

Dragons of the Slavic diaspora are able to metamorphose between forms and alter their appearance to assume the qualities of animals – their favourites were snakes and rams. But it could work in reverse too. A horned dragon might arise from a ram, and the 'source' animal is reflected in the outcome. Carp were another favoured origin – eating their flesh was taboo in some areas.[7].

By the Christian era the dragon (now an evil creature in the eyes of the West) was also downgraded to a dim-witted monster. Slavic myths, such as the dragon tricked by the gypsy, or the Magyar tale of Tobias,[8] reflect this downgrading. The structure of these tales is similar and runs thus:

> Confronted by a fierce dragon, a gypsy uses his whiles to trick the monster. The beast sets the man several tasks to test his strength, such as carrying an ox, or collecting a huge oak for firewood. Each time the cunning man works things in his favour so that the dragon is fooled into completing these tasks itself. It collects the timber for firewood, an ox for cooking and water for the pot. Impressed by his apparent strength, the dragon accepts an offer to visit the gypsy's home. It even loads their provisions onto a cart. At the sight of his children running to greet their father, the gypsy smiles slyly, explaining their delight is because they are hungry enough to eat a dragon. The creature flees and never approached another human again.

Chinese dragons are separated into four groups: there are the *jiaolong* or celestial dragons, which guard the Heavens. Then there are the *Shen Long,* or divine dragons which produce rain. The *Di Long,* are dragons of the earth, and the *Fu Zhang Long* guard hidden treasures. In ways these divisions echo those of the Indian Nâga.[9]

The idea of dragons as progenitors of rain, intrinsically bound to the elements of water is common in ancient Chinese culture. They live in lakes, rivers, wells and the ocean. From these they bring rain and sometimes floods. Adopted as symbols of power by sovereigns, they became guardians of dynasties and their presence was thought to establish balance and maintain the rhythmic order of life. James Fraser records that dragon parades in the country were a ritual prayer for rain.[10]

Although the dragon came to symbolise evil in the West, this wasn't always the case in the East, where it retained its benevolent character. Here the dragon possessed a profound level of meaning. It was one of the four supernatural entities that guarded the fate of China. There was also an azure dragon that ruled the East and was associated with springtime. As the yellow dragon it left the skies to sleep in its deep pool in the Autumn. Sometimes it appears in art with a human head and signifies the thunder god.[11]

As previously mentioned, there's a marked difference between the dragon of folklore and that of myth. The folkloric dragon in China is often portrayed as mischievous or evil. This type is also referred to as *jiaolong*. The tales about them are often influenced by Buddhism, which held an aversion toward the remnants of animist beliefs. This folkloric dragon was believed to be a tangible being that could be sought, fought and slain. Such an example can be found in the story of the hero, Cifei, who was crossing a river on a boat when two *jiaolong* drew alongside. Drawing his sword the hero exclaimed: "They're just rotten meat and bones" and leapt into the river, slaying the monsters.[12]

Where the peasantry felt the direct effects of an abundance or scarcity of water, then the folkloric dragon is prevalent. It was amongst the peasantry that, at numerous shrines across the land, the Dragon King was worshipped.[13] It was also said that rain came when you prayed for the dragons.

A Japanese legend relates that, while walking a bridge near Lake Biwa, *Tawara Toda* came across a huge dragon blocking his path. But Tawara was undeterred and simply clambered over the monster to get past. Looking back he saw that dragon had changed, becoming human-like and it wore a crown upon its head. This was really the Dragon King, who was rightly impressed by Tawara's courage. The Dragon King enlisted the hero's aid to kill a giant centipede that was terrorising his land. This Tawara did and in reward he was admitted to the Dragon King's kingdom beneath Lake Biwa. There he was given great gifts, including a never ending bag of rice, self-replenishing rolls of silk and a cauldron that cooked without the need for fire.[14]

In contrast, the treatment of the mythical dragon was different, it was abstract, formless, timeless, ancient and spiritual. The mythical dragons were hidden. They were rarely seen and they couldn't be fathomed. Their rare appearance meant that a great event would take place. In *A Journey to the West* Monkey asks the rain dragons to reveal themselves. There are four of them and they are soaring in the cloud. Their feet are clawed with white hooks and their whiskers are like white silk. They have clear-sighted round eyes and rugged foreheads.[15]

In their 'mythic' sense they are conveyers of profound wisdom and it is little wonder to find them in Taoist philosophy. Legend also has it that Fuh-shi received the inspiration for the sacred tetragrams of the I-Ching from the markings on the back of a dragon-horse that emerged from a river. In this divinatory process, the dragon was *Chen,* that is thunder. Many of the I-Ching's trigrams make specific reference to this elemental creature. But the dragon's link to wisdom does not end there, for another dragon conveyed Buddhist scrolls of law and dragons are also closely bound to the practice of *feng shui*. This ancient body of lore viewed the dragon as the primal active force, bound to the providence of all that the water element entails: creation, germination; the element vital to the harvest and growth and the sustainer of life.[16]

Here we get a sense that the dragon hasn't always been so maligned and, in its mythic state, it is intrinsic to Chinese culture. The country has a lengthy history of dragon veneration. During excavations near the Yellow River in 1987, a 6,000 year old dragon image was discovered. Even in the Bronze Age, two distinct types of dragons were recognised: *K-uei* and *Long*. The former is represented on the bronze vessels of the Shang and Chou dynasties, dating their appearance between 2000-1000 BCE.[17]

The veneration of the mythical beast can be traced far back into antiquity in other places too. In fact, possibly one of the oldest serpent-dragons in the archaeological record is dated between 9600-8000 BCE. This comes from the complex of Karahan Tepe, in Turkey. Situated 37 Km from Göbekli Tepe. The site is still under excavation. However, a series of three interconnected ritual structures have been unearthed there. They reveal a tantalising glimpse of the religious practices of these mysterious people. One of the structures, hewn into the bedrock, forms a shallow pool. Around it, carved along the base of a seat, is a long serpent. It's been suggested by researchers that the complex forms a ritual space. Another stone-cut cell, with ten pillars within it, had been intentionally shaped like that of a snake's head. A channel, grooved into the stone and through which water presumably flowed, forms the serpent's body. It's not difficult to see this place as part of a ritual that included purification, submersion and an association with serpent-dragon and water.[18]

Further afield the monstrous serpent is evidenced in Bronze Age carvings on areas of exposed stone at Bosulan and Ostwald in Scandinavia. Scattered amongst the many ancient images, huge serpents rove amongst sky-ships and cattle. One pictures two confronting each other (although in what context we can only guess). The majority of the carvings depict ships and sleds, of which many possess distinctive *dragonesque* prows – suggestive of the motif found in the later Iron Age and made famous by the Vikings (even though thousands of years separate these designs). In many ancient cosmologies, water is the source of all – the cosmic waters are the container for deities and worlds. It is worthy to note that many of these proto-deities are monstrous serpents and dragons.

Sesha was a Nâga king who ruled the underworld of Patala. In purple robes he holds aloft a pestle and plough. The Nâga are an important element of the dragon-kind, and appear as half-human and half-serpent. Sesha encompasses time, as do many of the great serpent-dragons. In this respect he reveals his cosmic nature: the allegory of time eternal. This enduring symbol haunts us still, in the form of the serpent encircling the material world, tail clutched in mouth. To the Hindus, as to pagan peoples in general, time wasn't a linear affair: a view that portrays reality as sequences of moments from point Alpha to Omega. Time, to the ancients, was cyclical. The intuitive notion of life's natural cycle.

At the end of a span of 1,000 ages (*Kalpa*) Sesha destroys the world with a ritual purification, like a wild-fire through a forest, making way for new growth.[19] Numerous myths the world over mention similar cycles and the destruction of civilisation by the gods. Sesha is also famous for being the great serpent upon whose belly the god Vishnu reposes, adrift upon the primal sea. With a thousand hooded heads he enfolds the resting god protectively. He's also known as Ananta or Virupaksha and is sometimes equated with Vrtra. He is married to a serpent goddess named, Nâgalakshmi who is sometimes a personification of the Milky Cosmic Ocean. Like many cosmological serpents, Ananta carries the world, girding it like a belt.[20] Such imagery brings to mind the Scandinavian Jörmungandr, which surrounds the known world in their cosmological model, gripping tail in mouth like an ouroboros.

Egyptian legends also allude to cosmic serpents, such as Apophis and Sito. Another serpent deity of note from this area is named Shai, whose worship was incorporated into Hermopolis' cosmological scheme. Shai was a primal creator archetype, the prime source from which the Ogdoad arose.[21] This occurred because the Serpent originally dwelled in the primal abyss, Nun. Forming a sand bank in the chaos, so that he could rest, Shai noticed a bed of reeds. For whatever reason, Shai ejaculated over these, giving birth to Ptah, the supreme deity. He was also said to set the span of a life. As the centuries passed he became personified in god-form, and eventually became the Agathodaimon of Roman Egypt. Shai was incorporated into the lives of ordinary people as a personal *daimon*, and was also seen as an element of the soul, as much as the *Ka* was too (the Egyptians believed that the soul was comprised of different elements, the *Ka* amongst them). He was equated with Helios by the Greeks, though his name in Greek translates as Psoi which was used to mean Agathodaimon. Shai was sometimes paired with a goddess known as Agathe Tyche and in this form their names are interchangeable with Dionysus and Isis. They appear as crowned Serpents with human heads.[22]

More examples could be pulled from the vast archive of human history here. Suffice to say what we are seeing here is how intrinsic the serpent-dragon was to human ideals and thoughts. Here it is far removed from the repulsive creature so derided by Sky God creeds.

Dragon Slaying Saints

Many Christians sought an expanse of the wilderness to commune with their god. However, these hermits also shared their solitude with the dragons of old. Evangelising Christians too found a land that was rife with the worship of 'devils' and 'dragons'. It is little wonder that, as literary subject matter, the medieval dragon became fodder for many a dragon-slaying knight. To a large extent these tales were fuelled by the imagery of the ever-popular St. George. This semi-mythical character became a Christian icon, and his image graces many a cathedral and church across Europe and beyond. The English relocated the myth of St. George to Dragon's hill in Berkshire, and the site of this legendary battle was evidenced by a patch of bare ground, where no grass would grow. This, it was said, was where St. George slew the dragon and the blood of the beast had flowed, poisoning the land forever.

In fact the saint never came to England. He was born in the 4th century CE in Lydda, Palestine. Declaring that he was a Christian, *Georgios* refused to take part in pagan sacrifices. At the time the Roman Emperor, Diocletian, was busily persecuting

Christians (though he only succeeded in radicalising them further). Georgios was captured in Nicomedia and subsequently tortured and decapitated on the 23rd of April. The story that combines Georgios with the dragon didn't appear until 1275 CE, in a publication called *The Golden Legend*. In this account, the hero lived in Silane, Libya, and rescued a virgin from a dragon. St George wasn't the first of these dragon-slaying tropes, but he proved popular, being adopted as the patron saint of England not long after the Norman invasion.[1].

But why would Christians relocate a foreign saint to British shores? And why choose that location? The site of Dragon Hill is a chalk knoll that forms part of an ancient ritual landscape, which includes the Uffington Horse (suspected by some to be a dragon) and Uffington Castle.[2]. The hill was inspected by Dr. Jim Leary and Quest in 2015.[3] He and his team took two core samples and determined the mound to be natural, although there's still speculation whether the top of the mound was flattened for some purpose. A charter from the 10th century CE gives its name as *Eccles Beorh* (meaning 'Church Barrow').[4] This suggests that an old church once stood upon this prominent viewpoint, and that the mound was believed to be a barrow even in those days. It's likely that its siting was significant, and purposeful. Placing Christian temples upon pagan sites was a way of consecrating and appropriating pagan grounds.

It isn't alone. There are a number of 'dragon hills' in the British Isles.[5] Although folklore tends to assert these monsters were slain by saints, the fact is that many of these places bear archaeology that reveals their use in more remote historical periods. Drakeslow, Drakeshole and Drakeswall all derive their names from Drake, ie; dragon. Its suffix, *-low,* comes from the Anglo-Saxon, *hlaw,* meaning Hill or rise. Here we have an older form of Dragon's Hill suggesting that, at least in Saxon times, these places were known to be the lairs of dragons. There are a number of them dotted around

England (in Nottinghamshire, Worcestershire, Cornwall and Derbyshire).

Sweeping hundreds of miles north, Dragon Hole on Kinnoull Hill, sits on the outskirts of the city of Perth. A strange rite is recorded in the writings of Thomas Tullideph, who described scenes of merriment, with music and dancing taking place in the cave on the 1st of May, in the mid-1700s. This Beltaine ceremony apparently had links to the dragon, and was enough to cause Thomas, a moderator for the Church of Scotland, total affront. However, this wasn't the first time the Kirk had been outraged by these lingering pagan-like celebrations.[6] As far back as 1580, church elders in Perth elicited a specific act to be drawn up named 'The Act of Dragon Hole' which stated:

> *"The said assembly wyth consent of the magistrates of this toun hes statut and ordanit that no persons heirefter of this congregation, nether man nor woman, resort to repair hereftir to the said draggon holl as they have done in tymes bygane, namely in ye moneth of May..."*[7]

Despite the edict, the revelries were still continuing hundreds of years after (and probably had been upheld centuries before this). As for the dragon of the 'holl,' it's been speculated that the monster in question is one slain by Saint Serf in the 6th cent CE. The saint, also known as Sevanus, was allegedly a son of the king of Canaan, who left to train in Alexandria and Rome, before making the voyage north. The Pictish king, Bruide mac Maelchú, himself already Christian, allowed the monk to set up a monastery in his lands.[8] However, popular tradition accounts the dragon he slew was actually in Dunning, Fife.

Brittany is well known for its connections with Arthurian myths. One romance tells of how the famed king arrived at the bay of Lieue de Grève, where a dragon lived in a cave. Joining forces with an Irish monk named Efflam, they battled the dragon for three days. It was a terrible monster, with a lone red eye glaring from its forehead, black scales and a maw crammed with curved tusks. There was no fresh water near the salty bay, until Efflam drew forth a welt of water for the warriors. He did this by beseeching his Lord and tapping a rock with his sceptre. The monk also overcame the dragon with prayer, proving to the king that force doesn't solve everything.[9] Another Saint, Pol, destroyed a dragon on the island of Batz by placing his *stole* around its neck and commanding it to disappear into the ocean; a command which it could not disobey.[10] France also holds its share of wells dedicated to dragons, such as *Foun del Drac* in Lozère.[11]

Another character associated with Brittany was Arthmael: a prince born in Wales but raised in Brittany.[12] He's said to have fought a battle against one of the *Dumnonii* tribe, slaying their king, Conmore. For this service Arthmael was bequeathed land. He became a Christian and set up a monastery in what's now the village of *San Armel*. The story goes that once the monastery was built, a dragon strode into the neighbourhood and started to cause bother. Arthmael confronted the monster deep in the forests, put his *stole* around its neck and led it to the river. There he commanded the monster to 'precipitate itself' into a river. The dragon obeyed, disappearing into the waters.

A similar tale connects dragons to springs and waterfalls and comes from the tales told of Guðmundur Arason, who is also known as Guðmundur góði. In the early 1200s he travelled around Iceland, sanctifying its rivers and springs. At Holme he even captured a serpent below the waterfall. This dragon was known as *Skirimsl*, and he sent it packing to the ocean, never to return.[13]

The fact that the majority of *pagani* held the serpent-dragon with reverence was a source of consternation to Church elders. It seems that the country folk tenaciously clung to their old traditions. Christianity's revulsion of the dragon was coded into its religious DNA.[14] Before the words of the Old Testament were committed to papyrus, its belief system had undergone a schism. The plethora of older deities were removed, as was any trace of Goddess worship. Instead the Hebrew sky god won favour: Yahweh. It was written in Genesis that the serpent placed enmity between the original human pair by tempting Eve and Satan was described as the 'Great Dragon'. These were central to the idea of human awareness and sin; upon which the Christian religion hinged. Their repugnance of both dragon and serpent (in essence the same) rippled from this congress. It didn't help that the image of the serpent permeated non-Christian beliefs.

Thus the dragon epitomised sinfulness and avarice to the Christians. They were monsters that dwelt in pagan wastelands, and it was the mission of saints to trample them beneath their feet. This is why there are many images of saints treading upon serpents and dragons around ecclesiastic sites.[15] The symbolism here is complex but negative (for the dragon). Though we must note that, despite the Biblical aversion to serpents, there are hints of serpent worship in the story of Moses. When he cast his staff upon the ground it assumed the form of a snake. He was also instructed to create a bronze serpent staff. This was allegedly worshipped in Jerusalem until the reign of king Hezekiah, in about 700 BC. The serpent god was known as *Nehustan* – a name said to mean 'brazen thing' or 'mere thing of brass'.[16] The king had the idol destroyed, although it had been worshipped for a thousand years.

In the British Isles there may well have been some form of syncretic blending of pagan and Christian beliefs within the Celtic Church. This early cross-over sect was known as the *Culdees*. They were the result of compromises, made by the first evangelists who infiltrated pagan Britain in the early Dark Ages. However, if this is so, there remains no literary remnant of such a belief. The only suggestion of such is the profusion of serpent imagery in Celtic Christian art. Monstrous dragon-like beasts also make their appearance, sometimes guarding the cross (itself often rendered in elaborate knot-work).[17] In this instance the cross takes on another symbolism, that of the Tree of Life.

Other, more benign examples can be found in examples of Pictish art, such as the Stone of Nigg, and from Iona (St Andrews Cross). We have to remember that these crosses were carved under the direction of local Christians. They suggest that Christianity was forced to make concessions with paganism to get its foot in the door. It may even be that early 'evangelists' were more accommodating, and some may even have been pagan priests before taking up the cross.

The instances of serpent-dragons in their art appear to be of a cosmological nature. They consist of serpents that spiral from great nubs of stone. Their inclusion in this form is highly significant and more suggestive of gnostic concepts, such as Ophism or the Naassenes,[18] than outright Christian. The imagery may even reflect themes of the early Christian scholars: both Clement of Alexandria and Bishop Porphyrius wrote that the soul took serpent form (and in this they were echoing pagan thought). A tantalising hint of gnostic and Druidic lore comes in the tale of the Druid, Mogh Ruith, whose name means, Slave of the Wheel. It's said that he travelled to the Middle East to meet with Simon Magus, known as Simon Druí. Magus was himself a renown gnostic and headed his own sect. He's remembered in the Bible in a negative light because he questioned the worth of Nazarene ideas.[19] If there's any truth to the legend of their meeting, could this interaction have involved the learning of gnostic ideas and their retrieval to the Celtic West?[20] Mogh Ruith's famed wheel, the *Roth Romach*, is mentioned in Medieval Irish texts as presaging doom and destruction. These texts centred around the apocalyptic date of 1096 AD. Reference is made to Mogh's wheel as also being a dragon.[21] *A dragon, in the form of a wheel* sounds suspiciously like an Ouroboros: a design formed of a dragon biting its own tail and a symbol that was used in gnosticism.[22]

It may also be that biblical dragons are veiled metaphors for how the Hebrews viewed their neighbours/gentiles. The Pharaoh was often called Tannin: a monstrous, tyrannical dragon.[23] Tannin is the same as Leviathan, the winding serpent and appears to be of the same mythical origin as Tiamat.[24] In Revelations, the imagery of the dragon was transferred to the enemy of the time, the Roman Emperor.

In fact, the dragon's fiery breath may also be a Christian addition. Fire purifies. It cleanses and allies the dragon with Hell. Fire is an unruly element that can't always be controlled, there's always an edge to it, always a possibility of great disaster. When fire is let loose it is uncontrollable and it roars as it rages, destroying whole towns. It was no random choice of the Christians to burn heretics, for burning was believed to eradicate sinful corruption from the world.

It also shouldn't surprise us that dragon slayers such as St Michael and St George were honoured as Christianity gained favour. Other dragon-slaying saints include, St Keyne, St Florent, St Philip and St Cado – but there are many more. The blazing wrath of Christian fervour is evident in the myth of Saint Margaret, who was imprisoned after refusing to marry the governor of Antioch. A dragon appeared in her cell to frighten her from her righteous path. Some legends say it swallowed her, but after making the sign of the cross she miraculously emerged from its mouth. Other tales say that the cross she brandished was enough to make it burst into flames.[25]

In Armenia many images of dragon-slaying saints occur throughout the Medieval period. They are sometimes conflated with historical personages, usually those that were bad rulers, those associated with devilish forces, or pagans. The Ruler, Pap Arshakid (ruled 370-374 CE) was despised by the clergy because he enacted anti-church reforms. It was said he was possessed by demons that slithered around his body in the form of white snakes.[26]

The alleged meeting between the recently converted Constantine, and the first Armenian Christian king, Tiridates III, is shrouded in speculation and myth. It's interesting to note that the spear given to the Armenian king had allegedly been dipped in dragon's blood, therefore making it able to penetrate stone and the skin of other dragons. This might be a thinly guised symbol of the need to convert the *pagani*. One of Tiridates notable moments was after becoming infatuated with a beautiful maiden named, Hripsime. She refused his advances and was thus roasted alive, and he had the entire cortege of nuns she'd arrived with slain. Hripsime was martyred. Soon afterwards Tiridates fell into madness, cavorting around like a rabid boar. He was converted to Christianity by Gregory the Illuminator (who Tiridates had previously imprisoned for thirteen years in an underground dungeon). Tiridates then commenced upon a crusade to bring his faith (he was of the Appian Christian creed – later considered heretical) to the people, and brutally put down the Zoroastrian faith that had flourished in Armenia for centuries. Destroying temples and shrines, he appears to have redirected his innate brutality upon the Zoroastrians – so much so that part of the reason so little is known about older Armenian religions is because, as well as destroying places of worship, he burned hundreds of texts. He was poisoned in 330 CE by rivals. With hindsight the character that Tiridates portrays bears all the resemblance of the personification of the dragon in its negative aspect: an aspect often superimposed on tyrants and dictators of the past.[27]

As for serpent-slaying saints, perhaps one of the most symbolic is that of Saint Patrick. He is credited with driving all the serpents out of Ireland. In fact, there have never been snakes or moles in the country. Despite the scientific realities that explain their absence, the symbolic reference is obvious. Across the length of the country, Patrick is credited with banishing and slaying dragons. Lough Muskry, in the Galtee Mountains was once known as *Loch Beal Dragan*, the Lake of the Dragon's Mouth. A Dragon called Ol'Nag was sent here in exile by the saint. He bound it to a rock in the lake with iron chains, promising to release it on an Easter morning after seven years. The folk story has it that every seven years Patrick returns to the well and the Dragon peeps its head from the waters, hoping to be set free. The same story is told of nearby Lough Diheen (it's possible the tale has become confused – or that each Lough once possessed its own dragon).[28]

Here we see that Christianity has a long dragon-slaying pedigree. However, this lineage was nothing new. If anything the essence of the idea was appropriated from an earlier strata of mythology, albeit to its own ends.

Now we must plunge into the pool of time. We must reach through the murk to glimpse older saurian legends drawn from the dawn of civilisation itself. We must now examine the greatest battle of the oldest war.

Chapter 2

The Oldest War

One thing that is evident from our investigation, is that there was a lot of enmity towards the dragon. Dragon slayers strode across the countryside, sword in hand to deal each dragon a few deadly strokes.

One of the Earliest Dragons in mythology is Tiamat, the Queen of Dragons. She is mentioned in the *Enūma Eliš,* which retells the stories of the Mesopotamian creation story and of the Great Battle between Tiamat and Marduk.

In the Beginning, Apsu and Tiamat created the gods and their children grew inside the belly of the great mother, Tiamat.[1] Apsu complained about the noise his children made. He wished to destroy them so he could rest – a suggestion which made Tiamat seethe with anger. She would not allow the death of their creations. However, Apsu's vizier, Mummu, counselled otherwise. Pandering to Apsu's intolerance they plotted to kill the young gods, but their clandestine plans were exposed.

The great god, Ea, rose up against the conspirators. He used magic on Apsu, making him drift off into slumber and then he slew both Apsu and Mummu. Ea then set up a great palace within Apsu's corpse, called the Apsu-home. There he joined with Damkina, who gave birth to the hero god, Marduk. Anu, the goddess of the sky, created the four winds and placed them in Marduk's hands.

Enraged at the murder of her mate, Tiamat made ready for war. She birthed an army of dragons, each cloaked in mantles of deathly rays. She also made eleven terrible demons, including the horned serpent, *Mušhuššu* and the *Lahmu*-hero, *ūmu*-demons and such. From their ranks she promoted Qingu to command them and took him as her lover, setting him upon a throne. In this way she became known as Queen of Dragons.

When news of his mother's war preparations reached Ea, he petitioned his father for help. But Anshar rebuked his son for stirring up Tiamat in the first place – after all, it was Ea who'd slain her lover. So Ea went forth to confront Tiamat alone, but she terrified him so much that he turned back, imploring his father to send another against her army, but all those chosen also panicked and fled.

Anshar convened a counsel and they made Marduk absolute king. With bow and mace Marduk set off in his storm chariot, showering lightning before him. He ensnared Tiamat within a net, using the four winds to contain her. Creating another three winds to help him, he then drew Tiamat into single combat. He put the *imhulla-wind* inside her, so she couldn't close her mouth, and pierced her belly with a great arrow, splitting her in two and slicing open her heart. Victorious, he stood upon her corpse while her army fled in terror.

From Tiamat's monstrous cadaver Marduk fashioned the sky and earth, forming order from the chaos of her body. He destroyed the Apsu home, erecting new temples to the lesser gods. Then he asked whoever was responsible for the war with Tiamat to be found. Qingu was blamed, hunted and brought before him. Marduk slew him and, with Qingu's blood Ea created mankind.[2]

So the story goes. A tale harking back as early as 2000 BCE – although in all likelihood much older. The popularity of the sky and storm god, Marduk, appears to coincide with the reign of Hammurabi, of the 1st dynasty of Babylon (1792-1750BCE). But Marduk's worship is more ancient, reaching as far back as 3000 BCE. His name means *the bull-calf-of-the-sun,*[3] a fitting appellation for a storm god.

The tablets upon which the *Enūma Eliš* is written are dated to the era of king Nebuchadnezzar (1124 -1103 BCE), though some scholars favour the earlier date of 1800-1600 BCE – a date which coincides with the rise of Marduk's popularity and may explain why it was written down at this time.[4]

It would be plausible to reduce the tale of the Great Mother, Tiamat and her overthrow to religious upheaval or matriarchal suppression by patriarchal incomers – but Apsu and Tiamat were originally envisaged as a male-female pair, their waters mingled together as they brought forth a lineage of gods.[5]. The favoured gods and heroes of the early Mesopotamian city-states waxed and waned. Invasions shifted the popularity of each city's patron deity like the ebb and flow of silvery tides beneath a gibbous Moon. Sometimes an enemy state snatched favoured statues of the deity, taking them home, only to have them snatched back at a later date. In this way idols became figureheads and were even believed to be vested with power in themselves.[6]

It's interesting to note that the aforementioned Nebuchadnezzar re-built a wondrous temple known as the *Etenanki*. It was known to the Greeks as the Temple of Belus (another name for Marduk). And was reputed to have been located next to the site where Marduk slew Tiamat: a spot of great significance, for it lay at the centre of the Babylonian world and crux of the universe. Indeed the temple was one of the largest ziggurats in ancient Mesopotamia. Its name is telling, for *Etenanki* means 'Platform of Heaven and Earth'. This magnificent building was described in a later cuneiform tablet as being ninety-one metres on each side and in height. The seven levels of this complex towered above the plain. A triple gate connected the temple with the *Esgila*, the building said to have been erected by Marduk himself, on the very spot where he slew Tiamat. It is the *Etenanki* that is referred to in the Bible as the Tower of Babel.[7]

Tiamat is much more than a one-dimensional antagonist and adversary for Marduk. Some refer to her as representing the saline waters of the ocean, while her consort is fresh water. [8] An echo of this early myth remains in Biblical sources that tell of, "the water which is above Heaven is male, and the water under the Earth is female." In the Bible, Tiamat is called *Tabaet* and more references are drawn to her serpent nature and association with water. She is also *Leviathan*, the female serpent who dwells in the darkness of the sea – however, her connection with the earth is snatched away by the all-powerful Yahweh, and she is reduced to a thing of evil to be despised.[9] This also parallels the relationship between the Greek Titans, Okeanos and Tethys. It's interesting to note that, as far as generations of deities are involved, Apsu and Tiamat are *titanesque* in nature. Both are usurped by the younger generation of 'gods'.

Apsu then is the male element,[10] Tiamat the feminine. According to the *Enūma Eliš* they sire the race of gods (sealing their doom): their waters mix and the creative process is begun. In Hebrew myth, *Tehom* is the feminine part of the primal waters, *Elohim* the masculine. In this chaos (*tohu-vabohu*) three elements flow together, creating order.[11]

However, Tiamat is also a mother goddess, a creator and designer. Despite her destruction at the hands of Marduk, her name was honoured. As late as the 1st millennia BCE, effigies of Tiamat's monstrous brood were regarded as possessing protective qualities, able to ward off malcontent and evil.[12]

In 250 BCE, a priest of the temple of Bel-Marduk, named Berossus, recorded a history of Babylonia[13]. Though his text is lost fragments survived, quoted in the writings of other scholars. What he is purported to have written is of interest. Despite the slightly garbled content, he records a startlingly familiar mythos to that relayed in the *Enūma Eliš*. Berossus tells of a creature called *Oannes*, a strange merman being, who flopped onto land and began teaching the primitive people agriculture, arts and science[14]. He went to work, compiling laws, building temples, cities, and, in short, civilising the barbarians. *Oannes* is said to have told of the World's origin:

> *Once there was a dark abyss of waters, wherein resided the most terrible of beings. These monsters were hybrids of the two-fold principle, man and woman fused together, and also mixed with beasts. Some with goat legs, or horses feet, some like hippocentaurs, or reptiles.*[15]

Images of these inhuman monsters were said to have been preserved in the temple of Belus at Babylon, presided over by a priestess known as Omoroca (*Thalatth* in Chaldean,[16] *Thalassa* in Greek). According to Berossus, this name meant either 'sea' or 'moon'. Out of nowhere strode Belus, savagely slicing Omoroca in two, forming the earth from her lower half and with the other the heavens. The monsters contained within her were slain too. Belus then struck off his own head and the other gods (presumably lurking in the backdrop somewhere) rushed forward, mixing his divine blood with the newly formed earth to create mankind. Here, Belus is likened to Jupiter: who created order from the chaos.[17]

The ancient battle between Marduk and Tiamat is apparent in the Berossus' tale, yet it is told almost two thousand years after the *Enūma Eliš* was created. It reveals an obvious continuity, even if names are different. There are also some interesting assertions in this text: the beasts that exist within Omoroca (ie: Tiamat) are recognised as possessing a two-fold principle. This notion of beings or objects (such as cosmic eggs, for example) containing both masculine and feminine properties is a reoccurring theme in pre-Christian thought.

In truth there were many Bels and Ba'al's for, as the name means 'Lord', it was added as an epithet to the diaspora of deities, e.g.; *Ba'al-zebul*, the Lord of flies (whom we know today as Beelzebub). Sometimes Lord (or Lady) was used instead of the true name of the Deity.[18] Marduk was also known as, Bel,[19] for to use the god's true name was viewed as profanity.

The ancient cult of Ba'al was the biggest threat to the early followers of Yahweh,[20] (YHWH) of the ancient Israelites. He also bears many similarities to the Christian 'Lord' of the first Testament. We must remember that originally Yahweh was one among many and a subordinate of El. They even fought the same deities.[21] Rahab, Tannin and Leviathan.[22] There's a strong case to be made that in Yahweh's rise, elements of older gods, whose popularity waned, were assimilated into the corpus of the mono-god.[23]

From the Canaanite city of Ugarit, texts dated to 1400 BCE reveal Ba'al as the son of the father god, El, and lady Athirat (Asherah).[24] Ugarit texts tell tales of Ba'al's battle with Mot (Death) in which he boasts of defeating the 'encircling' serpent with seven heads.[25]

Given the precedence of seven as a magical number in Babylonian mythology, it's of interest to note the reference to a seven-headed monster featured in other myths – such as that of Ningirsu (Ninurta) who also killed one. Could the seven-headed beast of the Bible be a piece of anti-Babylonian religious propaganda of the Old Testament, later interpreted as Anti-Roman sentiment?

The tale of Tiamat finds parallels in India, with the monstrous dragon known as Vrtra – the enemy of the god, Indra, and is described as 'shoulderless" (without arms or legs). Named as an entity of living power, Vrtra was the first born of dragons. Some say it was a Brahman, others say that it was born to the snake god, Danu, and therefore a *Danava*, or demon. It dwelled in the underworld, in a fabulous palace. Like Tiamat, Vrtra was envisioned as a monstrous serpent-dragon, whose name can be translated as 'the one who held back', or 'the restrainer'. In essence it is 'that which enveloped' a translation which gives the impression of the primal waters of chaos, encased in the shell of the cosmic egg, the pregnancy and potentiality of life longing to break free in a gush, restrained by the thin membrane surrounding it.[26] The imagery also brings to mind entities such as the Egyptian Sito.

Indra is Vrtra's destruction: a sky god who reigns over the mid-air regions between heaven and earth. He parallels Marduk and shares many of the qualities of other storm-Deities, such as Zeus. He's also equated with Ba'al-Hadad. Indra himself replaced an older storm-god, called Vaya, and his name may be a later corruption of Inmar; a sky god of Uralic speaking steppe nomads who are said to have been part of the 2nd wave of Indo-European migrants into the Indus Valley. Indra, god of storms and battles (sky god, warrior-god), rules over his kingdom alongside Agni, who rules over earth, and Sûrya, who lords over the heavens. They form a trinity of powerful deities, presiding over the three portions of Vedic space.[27] Indra drank the sacred *soma* and fought terrible demons.

One tale tells of how he slew a youth, Visvarûpa, the son of Tvashtri, *the divine artisan*. This inhuman child had three heads: one that drank the sacred brew, *soma,* one that ate spirit, and one that ate food. His name translates as: all-shape, all forms, true-form, omnipresent, universal. Indra hated the youth and struck off his heads with a thunderbolt. From the gushing wounds Vrtra emerged, swallowing Indra's cloud-cattle. Swollen with the Storm God's herd, the creature grew, blocking all the rivers with its coils, slurping up all the water with its maw. Only Indra was unafraid. He reigned down his thunderous fury and slew the dragon.[28] Visvarûpa is also mentioned as being a triple-headed dragon.[29]

In a version found within the *Stapatha-Brâhmana,* Vrtra was the direct result of Tvashtri's rage. In punishment for his son's murder, Tvashtri excluded Indra from the sacred *soma* ceremony – but impetuous Indra drank the sacred brew anyway. Incensed by this further act of arrogance, Tvashtri kicked over the tub of *soma,* spilling the dregs. Vrtra rolled forth, knowing all sciences, all glory, all nourishment and all prosperity. As it splashed upon the sacred flame of Agni, Vrtra took on serpent form, growing in size, becoming all consuming.[30]

Vrtra was taken in by the deities, Danu and Danáyû.[31] Indra then called upon Sûrya and Agni for aid, bribing them with promises of sacrificial honours, and they agreed. With their help, Vrtra was overcome by Indra's thunderbolts and its powers of knowledge became his. In this version the dying Vrtra pleads with Indra not to annihilate it, but sever it in two. Whichever the telling, when Vrtra was slain the waters of creation rushed free. He formed the sky from the upper part of the dragon's corpse; the lower half he used to form the earth.[32] This parting of the primal serpent is a theme that reoccurs in other myths:[33] the monster is slain to become the material plane of existence. By slaying the dragon, Indra ushers order from chaos.[34]

One school of thought suggests the myth describes a real event: a power shift between two competing cultures; that of the Harappan civilisation, which flourished between 2600-1900 BCE, and a wave of Indo-European invaders. However, this theory, popular in the mid-19th to mid-20th century, has fallen from favour. Archaeological discoveries, alongside DNA testing, recalibrate our understanding of the movement of peoples and cultures. It now appears that the Indus valley cultures were the result of indigenous tribes whose legacy stretches back in time to at least 6000 BC.[35] The ruins of Harappa haven't revealed archaeological evidence of the destruction expected from such an invasion.

However, it seems likely that climatic change may have ushered in the decline of the Harappan civilisation. A period of intensely dry weather, between 1900-1300 BCE, led to drought and floods. As the Saraswati River began to dry up this led to a lack of resources.[36] This environmental change also coincided with the decline of the Harappan civilisation, as populations moved to more suitable areas.[37] A body of evidence supports a migration of settlers from the area relocating in the River Ganges plain.

Trade existed between Mesopotamia and the Indus valley as early as 2500 BCE, and during this time a series of thriving trade routes were established. Along these roads towns flourished. There were two main routes, one of which would become the Silk Road, while an oversea route existed too, following rivers and the coast, crossing the Gulf of Oman. Turquoise, copper, chlorite, silver, alabaster, steatite and aragonite were traded back-and-forth between these cultures over thousands of years. With trade ideas travelled too.[38]

The ancient city states, such as those in Mesopotamia, or those of the Harappan culture of the Indus Valley, didn't happen overnight. They evolved around meeting places and trading settlements. The settlements of the Indus tradition were surrounded by walls of mud brick, but there's little evidence to suggest major conflicts existed within the culture (in contrast to that of Mesopotamia) and the walls seem to serve the purpose of regulating trade via city gates. Order and structure were required to maintain the city. Archaeological evidence of this order reflects a highly sophisticated 'mathematical standard' used throughout the settlements of Harappan culture. As far back as the earliest periods of its history (2800-2600 BCE), cities like Harappa (which covered more than 25 hectares) had a ground plan orientated to the cardinal points. Such systematic layouts are mentioned in Vedic literature, hinting at the establishment of Vedic concepts at a very early period. Whereas evidence is lacking for an overall elite, it could be that a common ideology was the mortar that bound this society.[39]

Could it be that the Vrtra myth reflects the environmental change that affected this society? In the Vedas, Vrtra is said to have blocked the rivers, halting their flow and causing drought. Is this why serpent imagery appears later in India, while precious little comes from the ruins of Harappa? Was this myth a way to explain this catastrophe? Or is such a rational explanation too convenient, too coincidental?

The *Vedas* are the texts that originally mention the first born dragon. Conservative estimates place their origins at around 1200 BCE. However, this date has been disputed by some scholars. Some point to the fact that the Saraswati River is mentioned many times in the *Vedas,* where it is described as a great flowing river, and yet, by 1200 BCE it was barely a trickle.[40] To some, this suggests that the age of the *Vedas* is much earlier than Western Scholars agree. The corpus of *Vedic* texts took time to become coherent systems of philosophical thought and must have existed in some form prior to the collection we know today. However, I think it is fast becoming obvious that such ideas aren't solely born from practical events. The battle between Indra and Vrtra is more than the folk memory of some disaster.

This dragon slaying myth appears elsewhere too. They follow a phenomena German Scholars termed *Chaoskampf,* recognising the widespread mythical tales of chaos monster and sky god engaged in battle. The tale follows a hallowed trope, despite the different names. From ancient Iranian literature come tales of dragon slayers such as Garshāsp and Sām, who both slay dragons from watery origins. Before the myth of Tiamat there was the myth of Enlil whose tablets of law were stolen by Zu, a terrible dragon and a monster of watery chaos. Zu was slain by the Sun God, Ninurta. Whether this set a precedent for other myths in the Indo-European pantheon remains to be answered. In Egyptian legend, Apep harried the sun-boat as the solar deity, Rĕ tarried through the underworld. Rĕ appointed Seth to protect him on the sun barge as they passed through Apep's domain. Apep is the night, but also the long night, it is death, the Underworld – against whom the Sun God engages a ceaseless battle. Apep is the serpent of chaos, disorder. He was also known as the World Encircler. Variants of his name include *Apepi, Aapep*. It is portrayed as an opponent of light and of *Ma'at* (truth/order). In this form, Apep is believed to have featured in

Egyptian myth from 8th dynasty onwards (2181–2160 BCE). His name survived in Coptic as *Apoph*. His hieroglyph is an eight looped serpent.[41]

The Hittite *purulli* festival celebrated the defeat of the dragon, Illuyankas by the storm god, Teshub. There are a couple of variations of this story, both inscribed side-by-side on clay tablets by a scribe called Kella. One tale relates how the goddess Inara invited the dragon and its offspring to a feast. They became so fat on the food and drunk on the wine they were unable to return to their holes. The serpents were bound and the storm god killed them. In the second version Illuyankas defeated Teshub in an initial confrontation. He claimed the storm god's eyes and heart as trophies. Teshub married the daughter of a peasant. Their son grew up and wedded the dragon's daughter, becoming instrumental in the downfall of Illuyankas.[42]

Perhaps one of the most well-known dragons of the mythology of ancient Iran, Armenia and neighbouring countries, is Ahi Dahaka. In fact even in the Rigvedic texts, Vrtra is called *àhi-dāsa*, or Azhi-Dahaka[43] – the name deriving from *àhi*, 'serpent', while *dāsa* can mean 'enemy', 'demon' or 'barbarian'.[44] In some interpretations Ahi is the son of the serpent god Danu and Vrtra.[45] Elements of the tale are found in the Avesta and later Persian fables. The popularity and fame of this dragon was wide and spanned centuries. Each culture offered its own hero and legend in the battle with this beast. The general consensus though, was that this dragon had six eyes and three heads and a body filled with lizards and scorpions.[46] Sometimes it appeared in human form with serpents rising from his shoulders. Ahi was defeated by the hero Vahagn in Armenian myth and Faridun (Thraetaona) in Iranian mythology.[47]

It was said that Ahi Dahaka reigned for 1000 years. It was a time of madness and terror. The sole purpose of the dragon is to snuff out the flame of life. Dahaka was overlord of a terrible army, including another dragon called Kundrav (Gandharva in

Sanskrit). This was something of a cunning character who acted as a spy for Ahi Dahaka. Other minions, held in the Dragon's thrall, were taught the necromantic arts by the beast.[48]

In the Persian version of the story, Ahi Dahaka's nemesis was Faridun whose origins can be traced to Thraetaona and to the ancient Iranian Deity, Trita. Faridun sought revenge for the killing of his father. Raiding the dragon's castle, he released the idol worshippers from their ignorance by teaching them the ways of the Zoroastrian god. After a short battle, in which the hero beat the dragon with his mighty club, the defeated dragon was dragged to Mount Damavand and imprisoned within (the hero nailing him with iron rivets to hang above a gorge, so that it would endure endless torment). Dahaka was already aware that it would die, for it had dreamt of the hero's coming. However, some have it that the dragon only sleeps within its stony prison. One day he will wake and break free. After-all, Mount Damavand is an extinct volcano.[49]

Mirroring Faridun, Vahagn is the ancient Armenian sky god, the product of the union of earth and sky. Comet-like he raced in his chariot across the heavens, marrying Astlik, the Goddess of the Stars. Together they populated the heavens with more celestial bodies.[50] Some worshipped him as the Sun. Vahagn was also known as Visapaklal, and in this form he was a dragon-slayer. He formed a triad with two other gods, Aramazd and Anahit. This trio bear a resemblance to the Persian gods, Mithra, Auramuzda and Anahita. His epithet is *vishapak'agh*, meaning 'He who Handles Dragons'.[51] He was also famed for overcoming Ahi Dahaka and binding him beneath Mount Damavand – thus he is the equivalent of the heroes mentioned above, and he is comparable to Indra. Vahagn was viewed as a force of good, and righteousness, embodying masculine hero concepts in fifteen symbolic aspects that included the boar, ram, young man and a fighting buck.[52] He is described as having fiery hair and beard with eyes like twin suns.[53] Like other Indo-European 'thundering' sky gods, Perkunas, Perun, Thor and Indra are also described having red beards.[54]

It's interesting to note here that much of the lore surrounding Azi Dahaka involves the dualistic faith of Zoroastrianism. This religion influenced Abrahamic doctrines, and appears to have been dead set against animist beliefs. Azi Dahaka appears to epitomise these more ancient concepts. However, as some tales maintain that he was never slain outright by Faridun, it is said that another hero will rise, reborn to confront the dragon when it wakes.[55]. Keresapa (also known as Garshasp) was a Zoroastrian-era dragon-slayer *par excellence,* famed for the slaying of the yellow-horned dragon, Ahi Sruuara.[56] But Keresapa displeased the divine lord, Ahura Mazda, after he joined the company of a witch called Khnathaiti. Guided by her influence, Keresapa returned to the worship of animist idols. For this crime he was sent to a purgatorial realm upon his death. There he sleeps, waiting for the day when Ahi Dahaka will break free and terrorise the world once more. The hero is thus fated to rise and confront the dragon in an epic battle.[57]

In Greek mythology, Cronus gave the Earth Goddess two eggs, smeared with his semen. These she buried (that is, placed them in her womb) and the resulting offspring was Typhon. Its sole purpose was to extract vengeance on the younger generation of gods for destroying the Giants. Another version tells that this mighty dragon was the offspring of Gaia and Tartarus. He was a fusion of fiery-eyed giant and winged dragon. His fingers appeared as dragon heads and from the waist down he was encircled by serpents. Of all the Olympians only Athena and Zeus remained to fight him, for the others assumed animal shapes and fled.[58] The battle took place on Mount Cassius, on the Syrian Turkish border.[59] Typhon overcame Zeus, wrestling his sickle from his hands. He then turned the weapon on its owner, severing the tendons of Zeus' arms and legs, rendering him useless. Then Typhon sealed the god in the Corycian cave, in Cilicia.[60] The dragon gave the god's tendons to the Dragoness, Delphyne but Hermes stole them and returned them to his father, restoring Zeus to health. The battle continued, raging around the eastern Mediterranean, until Zeus hurled Mount Etna at the dragon, trapping him under it. To this day the mountain still splutters with the remains of Typhon's fires.[61].

Apollo's removal of the Python from the sacred site of Delphi is one of the clearest of the Dragon-slaying myths. For, just as storm-browed Zeus slew the monster, Typhon, so his shining son Apollo was to kill Python: Desiring a place to make a temple for prophecy, Apollo chanced upon a spring of clearest water called Crisa. However, the Python dwelled there and needed to be dealt with first, so he slew her with an arrow from his bow. Not that Apollo was a stranger to Python. Hera raged at Zeus' for his adulterous union with Leto and she sent Python to pursue the pregnant goddess. The monster chased Leto relentlessly to prevent her finding a place to give birth. Python failed in her task and Leto gave birth to the divine twins, Apollo and Artemis, on the island of Delos. Years later, after slaying Python, Apollo crowned himself with bay laurels and swilled the blood from his hands in the River Peneus.[62]

The festival of *Septerium*[63] celebrated Apollo's conquest over Python and was held every nine years. The festival included the erection of a bay-leaf hut representing the first temple, which was ritually burned by a youth selected for the task. After the burning the celebrants left the site without looking back. The youth was purified with sacred water and then returned to Delphi along the sacred way.[64]

Hesiod, writing in *Theogony,* informs us that Python's assassination was more than a revenge killing. It was actually Telphousa, the spirit of another spring at Delphi, who told Apollo to create his oracle at Delphi. After slaying Python, Apollo returned to Telphousa and, for her help, ground a huge rock on her head. From a crack in the rock a spring issued forth, and another temple was erected on the site.[65]

It's worth noting the similarity between Python and Telphousa. Both are described as dragoness' or Drakainas. Telphousa is sometimes spelt Delphusa in translation. The character of Delphyne appears to be one-and-the-same.[66] Both are said to be buried under a rock: legend has it that Python was buried beneath the Omphalos, the sacred stone once reputed to be the centre of the known world.[67] Both are associated with springs, just as the Pythian serpent is connected to the river flowing beside the scene of its fight.[68]

Apollo replaced the Python with his own oracle, a priestess known as the Pythia. It was to the Pythia that people came from across Europe to seek advice. The oracle at Delphi was the most renowned of the ancient world, and the worship of Apollo there can be traced to the 8th century BCE, when his cult superseded an earlier sect.[69]

There is archaeological evidence to suggest that, in Mycenaean times, a cult associated with the earth existed at the site. Priests of the Apollon cult were normally men – thus, that the Pythia remained a female, points to some form of take-over of an established, and highly regarded cultic centre.[70] This event is thus memorialised in myth: Apollo undertakes atonement for slaying the Python, renames the new oracle Pythia in her honour, and a sense of the god's 'guilt' is reflected in the celebration of *Septerium*.[71]

Apollo is an interloper, a god who appears out-with Greece proper. A god of invaders. It is tempting to speculate that, in this tale, we have the recital of some historical event portrayed in a mythic context. The conquerors being associated with Apollo and his worship, the vanquished with Python and Telphousa.

Grecian god and hero Heracles happily mashes the heads and severs the necks of various dragons as he undergoes his labours. Geryon had three heads and lived on Erythea (sometimes it also had three bodies), and Ladon guarded the golden apples – until they met the club-wielding hero.[72] But these slayer myths aren't restricted to Greece or the Middle East. They range around the lands and we must track a few more yet.

The Scandinavian storm god, Thor struggles against Jormungandr, the great dragon that girds the known world. Thor went out fishing with the giant Hymir, and snagged Jormungandr, the World Serpent. He even managed to clear its massive head from the water, whacking it with *mjolnir* before the beast sank below the waves. At Ragnarok they will ultimately clash, with Thor smiting the dragon, but not before it bites him. The mighty hammer-bound god will take nine mighty strides then succumb to its poison. Jormungandr is often portrayed as a giant serpent, clutching its tail in its jaws. This is a symbol reminiscent of the ouroboros, and hints at the deep, cosmological nature of this world-serpent.

One of the most famous of dragons of early medieval literature is the unnamed beast that appears in a 6th century manuscript: *Beowulf*. Although penned in England, the story takes place in Denmark and in it, Beowulf's foe sits upon a treasure hoard within a burial mound. This dragon knows its horde intimately, right down to the last trinket – which is why it notices the theft of a small cup. Coveting its stolen treasure, the dragon begins to stew in rage until it can contain itself no longer. It lets loose upon the countryside, wreaking havoc and raging against civilised society. Beowulf arrives on the scene to finish it off, but the dragon's poisonous bite kills the hero. It is the hero's helper, Wiglaf, who actually delivers the killing blow to the beast.[73]

Then from the ends of the earth, a tale is told of a king of the *Ulaid*, Fergus mac Léti who was given supernatural powers by sprites he encountered at sea. These *Lúchorpán* gave him the power to pass under any body of water, except the lough known as Rudraige.[74] Reneging on this deal the king dove into the waters of the aforementioned lough. He came across a water monster known as a *muirdris,*[75] which was inflating and contracting like a smith's bellows – the sight was such a shock to the king that his jaw opened as far as the back of his head. This fact was kept hidden from Fergus, for no king with a blemish was allowed to rule the land. Therefore no one was to mention it and he was assigned a handmaiden to wash his face, lest he catch a glimpse of his reflection. However, a serving woman taunted the king after he was unfair to her (in another version she is his wife), and Fergus slew her and then confronted the *muirdris*. After a frenzied struggle, the king rose from the bloody waters, holding the monster's head aloft as he bellowed his triumph and then fell dead.[76]

I hope that these examples provide a non-exhaustive sample of this *Chaoskampf* phenomena. The story of the dragon slayer appears in many cultures, at various points in history. It is recorded in many tales of a gallant hero ranging forth to subdue an evil serpent-monster. Each time it's evident there is a distinct pattern: a theme that reoccurs with striking similarity between different cultures and at various times in our history. This theme is something echoed throughout these stories of the Great Battle, an event so great that it is imprinted in human myth in many cultures. This itself raises profound questions. Sometimes it feels like a conspiracy, echoing the notions of Marija Gimbutas, the archaeologist and proponent of the theory that patriarchal gods displaced matriarchal goddesses, relegating them to underground regions and reigning in their creative powers. Is this, in essence, what these myths suggest? A consolidation of tribal power? The dominance of the male, warrior-based Indo-European society over a more feminine, and gentler society that predated this. We shall examine these themes in a later chapter.

Chapter 3

The Benevolence of Dragons

The Dragon That Guards the Sacred Tree

Within the dragon-slaying myth it's evident that certain patterns are repeated. They appear in most of the myths, like constant refrains. Some of these shall be examined later, but for the moment we need to look at the corpus of dragon-lore to eke out other refrains. For each strand forms part of the song, from the tenor of battle, to the rising melody of the chorus. They all form the song of the dragon.

Armenian folklore tells of a youthful hero called Suren, who was adopted by a blind old couple. Three female dragons reigned over the land and it was these monsters who'd hidden the couple's eyes. In time, Suren met a speaking lion that gave him a pair of lion cubs. They quickly grew huge and remained by his side. Encountering the first of the dragon-sisters while watching the old folk's sheep, Suren wasn't beguiled by its request that he should comb its mane to search for nits. Instead he pretended to do so, but secretly bound the dragonesses' mane to a tree trunk. Then he demanded to know where the serpent had hidden his adoptive parents' eyes – she revealed that her eldest sister kept keys to a casket in which they lay. Suren promptly set his lions on her and they ripped her to shreds. Next he encountered the middle serpent, the same procedure followed: he bound the serpent and demanded to know the whereabouts of the key. The dragon told him that her little sister possessed the item. But, having already slain the youngest, the lie was exposed and Suren's lions disposed of her. Finally he encountered the third – the eldest – who was so large she blocked out the sun. Again she asked him to look for nits, and again he tied her to a tree. This time he took her key before loosing his lions. Then Suren retrieved the box and recovered the old couple's eyes so that they could see once more.[1]

The inclusion of sight here is interesting – having mentioned the origins of the word *Drakōn*, and its links to the idea of seeing. As shall soon be revealed, there's more to this than meets the eye (please excuse the pun).

Continuing the theme of three sisters a Czech folk tale tells of three doves, pursued by a dragon that was freed by an unwitting man. The dragon in the tale dwelled near the Red Sea, in a castle that had the ability to disguise itself as a horse. The doves were actually three princesses, cursed to assume bird-form for two hours every day. Under the dragon's thrall they were imprisoned in its castle. The dragon was difficult to defeat for it served the Devil's Grandmother.[2] This is none other than Baba Yaga, a magical old woman whose roots lay in deep antiquity. We shall hear more of Baba Yaga later on.

Straying further north, Scandinavian mythology reveals similar concepts, although convoluted and shadowed by time (as well as the religious bias of those who transcribed oral tradition onto parchment). Here a dragon gnaws upon the roots of the World Tree itself. This dragon, Nidhoggr, is associated with death and is awful in appearance – human corpses are threaded between his feathers and scales. Death is literally sewn into the fabric of its being. Nidhoggr dwells below the life bestowing world tree of Yggdrasil, and as his name suggests (Evil Below), he's up to no good. In this aspect the dragon is anti-life and carries with it a foreboding prophecy come the twilight of the gods. It might be that Nidhoggr is further incensed by the messages that the squirrel, Ratatosk, passes it from the eagle that sits atop Yggdrasil. All we know of these messages is that they are antagonistic. This interplay between heavenly eagle and underworld dragon, is suggestive of the constant strife between Sky God and Earth Serpent.[3] Despite its malignant nature, the siting of the dragon beneath the tree is significant. Yggdrasil is the vital centre of the Norse cosmology.[4] The base of this mighty ash is daily smeared with fresh clay from the well of Urð (Wyrd), signifying fresh layers of renewal. Three Fates, known as Nornir, gather around the waters weaving the destinies of all. Their presence links the tree to fate and to time itself. Yggdrasil harbours the many worlds and the Nornir are 'what has been', 'was will be' and embody the idea of 'becoming', or 'forming'. Although the Norse of the Iron Age believed in free will, it was only as far as destiny allowed: for a person's fate was already woven in the pattern of time. Through Yggdrasil the events of all the worlds and all time flowed, from and into the well of Urð. In most tellings there are three Nornir sisters (though sometimes there are nine – which shouldn't detract us too much as nine was a sacred number to the Norse: thrice times three maintains a triad as its foundation).[5]

I have already related the story of Apollo's slaying of the Python. Needless to say it is worth recalling that he also slew Delphyne and Telphousa: priestesses who were named Drakainas and were found at springs (and might well be the same being). Although Apollo slew them along with the Python, the site retained its sacred origins in a succession of Pythia's. Their oracle was the most famed of the ancient world. Here the idea of sight is relevant once again. To be an oracle is to be able to see, to gain prophetic vision. Both Drakainas have shrines at springs. Could it really be that what we have here, in essence, is a cult of the dragon, located at sources of water and involving oracular vision?

In Scotland, the tale of the Dundonian dragon is one that hinges on an old rhyme and introduces us to another link between priestess, dragon and well. The story goes that a farmer from outside the town of Dundee sent one of his nine daughters to gather water from a well, when she didn't return he sent out the next, on and on until all the sisters were gone. Martin, a young suitor of one of the girls, went to search for them and discovered them slain at the well, where there now dwelled a huge dragon. It was held that these sisters were buried in the Strathmartine kirkyard, beneath an ancient oak. The site of their alleged slaughter, at Pitempton Farm was known as the Well of Nine Maidens and was visited until the late 1800s, when the farmer blocked it off to keep people away.

Around the region folklore of Nine Maidens is recorded. The nine daughters of St. Donald were said to live not far away, in Glen Ogilvy. These 'nuns' were relocated to Abernethy. Nine Maidens, Nine Wells or Nyn Wells are recorded across Britain. Embedded in the lore of the land and its subsequent topography are clues that hint at a cult. A cult so important it wasn't above the early Christian apologists to incorporate scant elements of it into their own mythos.

In relation to the site at Strathmartine, there exist the remains of Pictish stones, more were mentioned in past records but they've long since disappeared. As it is, only a fraction of the symbol stones remain, due to ecclesiastical vandalism and neglect. However, the imagery of the stones is suggestive. One features a pair of serpents, entwined as though to form a spiralling motif. Another depicts the Pictish water horse, or Kelpie, alongside a detailed serpent that rests upon the so-called Z-rod.[6]

Are these images also linked with a cult associated with serpent-dragon worship? Could this same cult bear any relation to that at Delphi?

I feel we must explore the associations between the Nine Maidens and ancient lore a little more here. It was said that Nine Maidens travelled across from Ireland with St Bride. However, place names indicate that the veneration of Bride, most likely in her pagan form, as a goddess, were undertaken by Pictish peoples before their tribal identity was subsumed into that of the Gaelic speakers from the west.

Bride equates with the ancient Irish goddess, Brig, who was eclipsed by the personage of St. Brigit. But she was perceived as the springtime aspect of the goddess, a beautiful maiden whose arrival heralded more clement seasons, but whose demise ushers in her other half/aspect: the Cailleach, or winter crone. The Highlands of Scotland were once alive with her tales and, to compliment her folklore, place-names readily root her presence to the land – especially in the mountains with which she's equated. There is also a profusion of place names linked to either St. Bride or Bride – in Pictish territory her name often appears without the saintly prefix, suggesting an older strata of veneration and infers that she retained her popularity into Christian times.[7] She often appears in lore accompanied by nine priestesses.

Brittany was settled by people of Brythonic stock in the 6th century CE. It's possible that the mythic *Korrigan* is a version of the Welsh goddess, Ceridwen. Although Korrigan became a term to refer to a hag (just as *Carlin* did too), there exist stories in which she performs the role of a powerful magician – often in the company of nine sisters.[8] A legend from Brittany places Dahut, (either a heroine or a goddess, sometimes fused with the historical personage of Ahès; a 6th century CE princess) as an adherent of the 'old' religion, who enlists the help of powerful witches called Korrigans to build a fabulous city. This place was called Ys, and was located at the westerly tip of the Breton peninsula. The wizards were said to have come from the sea to build the city. Their creation was a marvel to behold, with golden walls erected by dwarves to hold back the waves. Dahut herself lived in a marble palace within the fabled city. The ocean provided another bounty in the form of dragons, whose powers Dahut harnessed to provide riches from across the seas.[9]

In the Celtic Sea, off the coast of Brittany, lies *Ile de Sein* – once the home of nine priestesses known as the *Gallizenæ*. According to the account given by the historian, Pomponius Mela, they were believed to have powers over the elements, and possessed shape-shifting abilities. Known to be healers, their island was a place where oracles were given.[10] Here we return to Dahut. In this version her father was king Gradlon, and his land lay between *Ile de Sein* and *Pont du Rez*. His city was named Ys (*Kêr-is* – the Low City). Large dykes surrounded it to protect it from the sea. The devil came to Dahut in the form of a lover, and he had the princess steal the keys to the dyke's gates, to prove her love. Besotted and biddable, she achieved the theft and the Devil opened the gates. Hence the kingdom of King Gradlon was submerged beneath the waves, though the king escaped (this is only one of several versions). For her part in the disaster, Dahut was transformed into a siren, and is associated with Mary Morgane. This latter appears to be a corruption of the Arthurian character, Morgan Le Fay who, according to medieval tradition, is buried on the island alongside Merlin. Two huge megaliths stand outside the *Eglise Saint-Guénolé,* locally known as the *Predicateurs,* or preachers. The stones may once have been part of a larger megalithic circle, and were erected between 6000-2500 BCE.

Ile de Sein is enthused with ancient archaeology, and around it much lore has gathered, including tales of Druids and hints of Arthurian myths. In the *Vita Merlini,* the *Insula Avallonis* is where nine priestesses dwelt. They were led by a figure known as Morgen. Much has been written about the origins of Arthurian myth, with authors making viable claims for the placement of the legend in this region or that. However, I believe that the Arthurian myth, its core players and themes, are much older than the claims of Dark Age warlords. Taking the legends of Fionn mac Cumhail as an example, which although originating in Ireland, were shared by people for whom the sea was a highway. Very ancient links were established between Ireland and the West of Scotland by coracle and ship. With the traders, fishermen and farmers, came stories. These stories became transplanted upon the features of the landscape. In SW Scotland there are many cairns named as Fionn's burial site.

Local communities and settlers wove the stories that meant most to them into the fabric of the land. Through lore, legend and language identity is maintained, balance is kept. The same is evident with the tales of King Arthur, Morgan le Fey, Merlin and Avalon.

Like the Gallizenæ, Morgen le Fey is a shapeshifter and healer. She presides over the mystical rituals that take place on the isle of Avalon. She is also accompanied by nine priestesses. Avalon denotes a land of apple trees, a place where fruit hangs upon the sacred trees of a sacred grove. This powerful figure attends the dying Arthur on the field of Camlann. It may well be that, as head of the nine, she is unveiled in her true essence. Morgan has been identified as the Gallic Matrona, one of the triple Mother goddesses (Matronae), whose statuary once spread across Europe. The Brythonic Goddess, Modron is equatable with Matrona. She is the mother of the Divine youth, Mabon. These links are important. They suggest that the priestesses might have also represented divine figureheads. (The link between Modron and Mabon does not end here – for the divine youth is paralleled in Irish mythology by Oengus mac Óg, whose mother is Boand and whose lore links her with the River Boyne and a sacred well – a story we shall examine shortly.)[11]

The raven goddess, Morrígan – sometimes portrayed as a triumvirate of Macha, Nemain and Babh – appears in much Irish law. She's traceable also in Gallic as *Cathubodua* (Battle crow). In Arthurian myth, one of the priestesses of the isle of Avalon transforms into a raven, and Morgan does appear to share elements of her name.[12]

It is told that Ruad mac Rigdonn, an Irish prince, travelled to Norway to meet with his allies. He was shipwrecked on an island and he discovered a secret land, beneath the waves where nine priestesses lived. They welcomed him, and bestowed him with many gifts of bronze and one priestess bore his child. He promised to return after his visit to Norway was complete, but reneged on his oath. The priestesses came looking for him, armed to the teeth and bearing aboard their radiant bronze vessel his son, now aged seven years. As they rode the waves in hot pursuit, it was clear they couldn't catch Rigdonn's vessel, and so the mother of his child slew their son, and ditched his body overboard.[13]

This particular myth isn't alone in its reference to the priestesses having martial qualities. Indeed, in the myth of Cú Chulainn, the youth travels to an island off the Scottish coast to be trained by the Amazon-like warriors, Scathach and Buanann.[14] Just as with the folkloric personage known as the Gruagach, we can detect here vestiges of a druidic female who trains youths in the skills of heroes. As described in the tale, 'Conal Gulban' in which a queen sends her children to be trained by the Gruagach of *Bhein Eidinn.*[15] In folkloric accounts the regal bearing of both a female and male Gruagach is asserted. As a powerful druid or wizard, the Gruagach appears in many old Irish tales and is often associated with the mythical *Tir na Sorcha* – the Land of Light.[16] To add more fuel to this rather inspired blaze, folklore from the West of Scotland holds that a '*Greogaca*' haunted the island of Troda, another was found on Inch, near Easdale Island. The folkloric Brehon faerie being. *Groac'h,* or *Grac'h,* is also a name for crone or hag with watery associations. Were these the folk memory of Druidesses (not entirely shorn of their power, even in remembrance)?[17] It's not difficult to see the relation to the Welsh *Gwrach* here either – a term for a mountain witch and also used in reference to the last sheaf of corn to be cut in the fields. A similar libation of which was left for the Cailleach in Scotland.[18]

This warrior status echoes Norse mythology regarding the Valkyries. These supernatural women escorted the dead from the battlefield, guiding them to Valhalla. Usually they were counted as being nine (although other accounts give less or more). However, their ability to shift into swan form echoes familiar themes of shape-shifting. In the Norse mythos, nine maidens also accompany the Goddess, Menglod. In her mountain hall (*lyr*) she sits with her maidens and they are well versed in the arts of healing.[19]

In the old accounts of Adam of Bremen, he mentions an Island of Women in the Baltic sea. These women are likened to Amazons and were said to worship dragons. Another nearby island, Estland, seems to have housed a similar cult, and we are told its women traded male slaves from passing traders to sacrifice to their dragons. The men were carefully inspected, as any blemish would result in the offering being rejected by the dragons. This Medieval reference is brief and tantalising. The Island of Götland also sits in the Baltic, and possesses a number of ancient serpent and dragon images. One of the most iconic is located at När Smiss, and depicts a squatting female who clasps two serpent-dragons in each hand. The heads of these creatures are markedly distinct. A triskele associated to the site is composed of snaky limbs that terminate in three different animal heads: a raptor, boar and dragon. However, whether these were in any way linked to a cult of women is uncertain.[20]

As we see, the presence of Nine Maidens, remains tangible in lore and legend. Are they goddesses, priestesses... or both? They tend to inhabit sacred or mysterious islands. This refrain is reflected in another branch of dragon mythology. In this strand dragons, maidens, water and islands remain, but another element appears: the sacred tree, with its magical fruit.

One version runs thus:

> There was once a place of natural beauty and innocence where nothing bit, nothing stung, and there was no cold or searing heat. In this garden stood a tree whose boughs were filled with ripe fruit. Sharing the garden with the animals were a human couple. They were as innocent as mannequins and they existed purely for the

> enjoyment of their creator: but it was a jealous god. They were warned not to eat the apples from the tree. In its boughs there lived a serpent and this cunning creature enticed the woman to eat the forbidden fruit – to open her eyes. Being inquisitive, the woman took a bite. Self-awareness filled her and innocence fell away. No longer Yahweh's puppet, she had the man eat of the fruit too. Incensed by their transgression, the tyrannical gardener expelled them from his paradise, placing at the entrance a cherubim guardian with a flaming sword to ensure they'd never return. He cast them out, into the world of Reality.

At least, that's how the Biblical version of the story goes. But we must ask ourselves; why did Yahweh tell the couple about the fruit in the first place? In fact why did it even exist? Why did he wish to conceal their true nature? Why couldn't he forgive them? And why did he allow this incident to excuse the persecution of females for thousands of years – relegated by the inquisitiveness of Eve to subservient status? In both Ophite and Christian texts, the serpent is cursed for gifting the apple to Eve – and she in turn shoulders the blame. By this act women are denigrated and marked as flawed, and all because Eve was open to the seduction of the serpent. It's difficult not to see this as pure patriarchal venom. In the Abrahamic religions we see an obvious distain of the female in the religious aspect. There is a sky god, but no earth mother. She is just 'woman'. Once there had been a goddess too, but Iron Age Hebrews cast aside female orientated cults.[21] This schism is alluded to in the Bible whereby Moses casts down his serpent staff and idol.[22]

In truth, the tale of serpent and tree is much older than the Bible. It is a tale that shifted and changed. Still, a pattern emerges that is frequent and telling. For example, there are similarities between the dragon lord, *Ningishzida* and the serpent that guards the tree in the Garden of Eden. Ningishzida, the ancient Sumerian dragon deity, guards the Tree of Life: a powerful deity who is privy to the knowledge of the heavens and the underworld. Just as the Christian Flood story occurs in ancient Sumerian stories of Utnapishtim, so too the Garden of Paradise existed in other forms – only it wasn't always a bad thing to partake of the fruit. In truth, the fruit of self-knowledge performs a vital role in many myths. The compilers of the Old Testament needed their doctrine to control their flock. Knowledge of the Self contradicted the position of the rising priesthood as it consolidated its religion, paring off as heresy that which didn't suit its needs.

Greek legends relate that in the Garden of the Hesperides golden apples grew upon a sacred tree. It was guarded by a horned dragon known as Ladon. The chronicler, Apollodorus, placed Hesperides in the lands of the Hyperboreans.[23] Others said the island lay beyond the Atlas Mountains, or on lake Tritonis.[24] Either way the garden was a sacred, secretive place: a paradise where a great tree stood, its boughs weighty with sacred apples. These fruits had been gifted by the earth mother, Gaia, to Hera when she married Zeus.

It was said that Hera herself placed the dragon in the Garden, and he was the immortal child of Typhon and Echidna. Although his birth is also ascribed to the incestuous liaison between Ceto (which means 'sea monster) and her brother, Phorcys. This would make Ladon kin to the Graiai and the Gorgons, while Echidna was also the birther of monsters.[25] Hesiod said that the Hesperides lived near the Graiai and indeed some ancient chroniclers reported that their parents were also the offspring of Ceto and Phorcys, which would also link them to the sinister ancient sisters.[26]

The Hesperides were said to watch over the sacred tree that sat above a double-mouthed well. They were daughters of Evening and Nyx. Their names were Aiglê (Egle), Erytheia (Erythea) and Hesperethousa (Hesperusa). However, sometimes more are mentioned, but most commonly they are three in number. The sisters protected the golden apples from the daughters of Atlas, who wanted to steal them.[27] We are told that the Hesperides sang and danced, and they embody the wonders of youth. Their neighbours, the Graiai, on the other hand, are gorgons: sinister creatures with only one eye and a single tooth between them. Their names reflect their nature, Pemphredo (Alarm), Enyo (Horror), Deino (Dread).[28] The inference that the Daughters and Ladon are related is of note. Could this hint at a deeper connection? If not sisters to the dragon by birth, then in creed: as priestesses who tend the sacred tree and well under the guidance of the Dragon?

There are a few versions of how Ladon met its end.[29] All involve Heracles, because 'scrumping' the sacred apples was on his 'to-do' list. In one tale the hero discovered that he couldn't collect them himself, so he asked Atlas to do the job for him. The exchange came at a price: Atlas would retrieve them if Heracles shouldered the burden of the world upon his back while the giant was away. In the other version Heracles slew the serpent himself.[30] However, the dragon was important enough to be subsequently transported to the heavens by Hera, to become the constellation of the serpent, Draco.[31] Other writers also define Ladon as a monster with a hundred heads.[32]. It was multi-lingual and ever-watchful.

Vestiges of a garden of paradise also existed in the Celtic stories of otherworldly haunts. These gardens were something of an afterlife, a realm of gods who kept great halls that were alive with banqueting and merriment. This land was inhabited by magical beings and filled with unearthly but wondrous places. In Irish tales these are the realms of the Tuatha De Danaan. This mythical race were the divine children of the goddess, Danu. From Celtic stories we know that in the 'Otherworld' there were sacred trees whose boughs were heavy with fruit of silver and gold. Sometimes such branches were brandished by the gods. In one such instance the God, Manannan mac Lir came to the land of humans bearing the *craeb-side*. This magical rod hung with silver apples and possessed powerful healing properties. The land from whence he travelled was known by various names, the most famous being *Tir na nÓg*, the Land of Youth. It was said that no sickness and no pain existed there.[33]

In the Celtic realms, when the sacred tree makes an appearance, it is often linked with a well. Sometimes the tree is a hazel, from whose boughs the fruit of knowledge (in the form of hazelnuts) drop into the sacred Well of Knowledge to be consumed by the salmon (of knowledge). Any that partake of the flesh of this fabulous creature will know all things. In the folkloric version of this myth a white adder dwells below the hazel's roots. Another cycle of old Irish and Scottish tales is associated with a hero named Fraoch. On the orders of King Ailill the hero swam to retrieve rowan berries from an island on a loch. A monster lurked within the waters and they engaged in bloody battle. The berries were said to bestow immortality.[34]

We know that Celts and Germanic tribes favoured sacred groves to practice their worship. The Roman writer, Lucan describes a druidic sanctuary in the south of Gaul which was populated by large oaks around whose trunks many serpents coiled.[35] There's also evidence that certain Celtic shrines were organised around a central post, possibly representing the *axis mundi*, or sacred tree. It's thought that some tribal names hint at a belief that they were descended from trees.[36] This isn't as wild as it sounds. In Scandinavian mythology humans are the descendants of Ash and Elm, brought to life by the Aesir. Another sacred garden was owned by the Norse Goddess, Idunn. In it she kept sacred apples coveted by both gods and giants.[37]

Time-and-time again we are seeing that these myths form part of a complex pattern that is repeated in various countries. The pattern forms a triad of *tree, well* and *serpent-dragon*. This tree is also the entrance to both the Underworld and the Heavens, and although it is guarded by a dragon, not all have the World Tree's best intentions at heart – and in this respect Nidhoggr isn't alone. The dragon which guards the Iranian Tree of Life also desires the tree's elixir for itself.[38]

In Rigvedic cosmology, there is a serpent of the deep known as Ahi Budhnyà – *àhi* means snake (as in Ahi Dahaka), *Budhnàs* means bottom. The word is also used in reference to the celestial root of the world tree known as *Nyagrodha* – confirming the serpent's link with the Tree of Life. Ahi Budhnyà's lair is within the infinite cosmic waters.[39] This primal abode mirrors that of Sito, the Egyptian primordial serpent.

According to Slavic folklore, dragons were known as *Zmaj* and dwelled in trees by lakes and rivers. A hollowed out beech was their preferred haunt. These were known as 'dragon trees' in local custom. Their proximity of water, and the nesting *Zmaj* in the tree, seem to echo the concepts already mentioned here. Another Slavic dragon, Simorg, may have its roots in ancient Persian mythology (he was still known to Ukrainians in the 10th century). Simorg is a hybrid cross between dog and bird – but how anyone could tell might be the biggest mystery, for Simorg was invisible. Its sole function was to guard the Tree of Life, from whose boughs hung the seeds of every plant in the world. This fearsome dragon protected it against woodsmen – for it was located within a great forest, but there was little to tell it apart from the other trees. Woodsmen performed elaborate rituals to safeguard themselves lest they accidentally attempt to chop it down. Simorg is sometimes depicted poised upon a tree that sits upon an island.[40]

The Kalmyk tribe, who live upon the Russian steppes, believed in a dragon that dwelled in the sea and watched over a sacred tree known as *Zambu*. Siberian Buryats held a belief that the Great Serpent, Abyrga, dwelled beside a tree that stood upon an island in a lake of milk. Sometimes it is the World

Mountain, *Sumur*, that he coils about, but in either case the myth is structured the same: there is a sacred centre on an island in the middle of a sea of nourishing liquid. Atop the tree lives the great eagle, Garide. This eagle is similar to Hindu, Garuda and the unnamed eagle that sits atop Yggdrasil. In Zoroastrian lore, the sacred *Gaolterena* tree grew on an island in the cosmic ocean known as *Vourukasha*. It was guarded by a giant dragon created by the arch-fiend, Ahriman.[41]

An ancient peoples known as the Sogdians played a key role in bridging the crossroads between Iran and the Near East, China and Central Asia. Their lands formed a vital hub, from which trade flowed east and west, north and south and is recorded as far back as 2600 BCE (and likely existed earlier). The Buryat are descended from these people so it's no surprise that their rituals contain refrains of Zoroastrian/Mithraic, or even animist ceremonies.[42]

Here we glimpse something older, hinting at the deep roots of this myth: there is a great, all-encompassing tree. Its boughs extend across the skies, and golden globes are suspended in its branches. At its base is a large, deep pool. From the waters a dragon watches. The tree is a spine upon which the universe is nested and within the boughs of its endless span worlds wait, galaxies rest. The spine of the universe extends through it all. Like a spine through a body. The branches are ribs and the worlds its organs. The dragon waits, coiled at the base of the spine, waiting for release.

The Abrahamic beliefs of Christianity and Islam incorporated this earlier myth into their symbolic codex. Although never referring to it in scripture, the world tree and its dragon are often alluded to. Early Dark age crosses across the UK and Ireland depicted images of a living cross, a Tree of Life. This imagery is clearly reflected in early pictorial carvings from 5th-7th centuries CE in Britain. Often flanking serpent-dragons guard the cross/tree. They bear a striking resemblance to carvings found in Armenian Christian imagery of the 12th-13th centuries CE, which were known as *khatchk'ar* and translates as 'wood of life'. All have their roots in common ideology which first makes its appearance thousands of years before the codification of Hebraic lore.[43]

Like the serpent chasing its tail, we have come full circle. The tree becomes the cross, and with it, the transference of a new set of symbols sets about it. This symbolism surely had to change, the serpent that guarded the apples and the conscious knowledge it offered is expressed as evil by Yahweh's Christian adherents. But the ideas referenced in these images were taken underground. Gnostic and Hermetic sects still honoured the serpent and saw this new god as a tyrannical imposter.

In the East the fascination with dragons was always mostly positive. For example, in China dragons served as emblems for emperors and dynasties. They were embroidered on the emperor's clothes and it was one of the four sacred animals that watched over the destiny of the Chinese people. A cursory glance through any book on Chinese art will reveal that dragons are a very common source of inspiration. The mythical Chinese dragon descended into the waters at autumnal equinoxes, rising again at the vernal equinoxes. Dragons were as equally at home in the upper realms as they were in the deep oceans, lakes and abysses. They thus bridged the realms of the heavens and the underworld. Therefore we can understand the Chinese reverence for them. The mythic dragons were not creatures to be hunted down and killed (unlike those of folklore). For why would you destroy that which gives life? They swam amongst the banks of cloud, creating water with their very breath, bringing both the gentle spring rains or full-on storms. As they rode upon water they were likened to gods. Sometimes they were portrayed clutching orbs or spirals. The spiral was said to represent the rolling storm. Here, dragons were symbols of fortune because they brought the rains that were vital for the crops to grow. Thus dragons were intrinsically bound to the idea of fertility and the principle of moisture. They can be seen as essences of life, intrinsic to the creation and stability of civilisation. In ancient Chinese mythology the cosmic ocean was seen as a progenitor of all. Water is necessary for life to exist, but this concept wasn't only restricted to China.[44]

The Japanese dragon is a symbol of storms, hurricanes and typhoons. Its imagery may well have been influenced by Southeast Asian mythology, before Chinese ideas entered the country. Japanese sea gods were often female water snakes, while their rain gods were identified with Chinese-style dragon kings. There's a link between the Nâga of India and the Japanese dragon mythology too. These foreign influences fused with local Shinto concepts, which already knew of water spirits in serpent form. This appears to have been the case in a description from James Fraser's Golden Bough. He describes a procession of villagers that took place in the 1800s, where a black dog was dragged into the mountains to be sacrificed in honour of the dragon deity of a river. The black dog epitomised the rain clouds that the villages wished the dragon to unleash.[45]

The Japanese sea god, *Oho Watsumi no Mikoto,* was serpent-like and had a palace in the depths of the sea (a refrain that echoes the Nâga).[46] However, the original Japanese dragons were named *Tatsu,* and were mostly ocean dwellers.[47] In India too, the link between water and dragons preserve a deeply magical and religious origin, echoed in the Vedic texts. Here the serpent was revered in many forms. As serpent spirits of wells and rivers they connected the people with the land, with fertility, life-bringing waters and immortality. The serpent was also known as the husband of all women. Indian Komati tribes used stone serpents to perform a ritual of potency for their wives. The form of the serpent is obviously suggestive of phallic imagery. Sometimes this potency was believed to be too powerful, and serpents were blamed for the menstruation of women.[48]

The Hydra (a dragon with many heads) was also said to symbolise sacred springs of the Grecian countryside. Perhaps this is a tantalising reference to the worship of wells associated with dragons. For example, Delphyne was known at Delphi, Telphousa guarded another nearby spring – both were referred to as *Drakainas*, ie; dragoness (though they might have been one and the same). Perhaps the Spring of Ares was such a place – it was guarded by a dragon set there by the war god himself, until Cadmus slew it. He subsequently founded the city of Thebes in the place where it was slain. Cadmus and his wife left the city after many years, to rule over the Illyrians. Later both husband and wife changed into serpents and went to the Elysium fields. Another tale has it that Cadmus was also instrumental in helping the wounded Zeus regain his tendons during his battle with Typhon. The spring of Ares was originally called *Ismenus*, after a river god, but before this was called Ladon – the same as that which guarded the golden apples of the Hesperides. Whether or not this was the same entity, it does suggest that they performed the same function: They were guardians. It's also notable that Telphousa was reputedly the mother of the Theban serpent.[49]

Armenian folklorist, Garegin Servantsian (writing in the 1800s) records that in ancient times, serpents sought a particular flower that grew near sacred wells and which, once eaten, secured their immortality. They would then shed their skins, bathe and sup from the well thrice and be blessed with eternal life. It was said those who performed the same ritual at this pool would also become immortal. Tales also tell of a sulphurous well at the ancient city of Palmyra, which belonged to a demon that appeared in serpent form. Other Syrian wells were reputedly guarded by spirits that took the form of pythons.[50]

Even in the Celtic story, *The Song of Wandering Oengus*, the divine youth, Oengus mac Óc dreams of a lover he is yet to meet. He wanders the world seeking this phantom, finally discovering her on the Lake of the Dragon's Mouths. There she glides in the form of a swan, bedecked in golden chains.[51] This lough is associated with other dragon lore, and we have seen that many Irish loughs do. I have also mentioned that the celebrated hero of Irish myth, Fionn mac Cumhaill, certainly battles his fair share of dragons. In Strangford Lough he encountered one huge beast whose head was as large as a hill, with teeth like tree trunks. Addressing the monster, Fionn and his men learnt that this beast came all the way from Greece to battle the Fianna. Announcing its lineage it claimed its true name was 'Height of Battle' – the climax of battle-frenzy. Regardless of its boasts, the beast was doomed to die beneath Fionn's spear. The hero then embarked on a tour of Ireland, ridding the land of serpent-dragons, phantoms and other monsters – most of these were found in loughs. Amongst them was the shining serpent of the Shannon.

The divine *Sinann* had everything she desired save *immas sóis*, the 'great knowledge'. She knew of a sacred well, from which seven streams flowed. Their waters sang with poetry, and it was said that the Wisdom of Segais was found under the well. Above the well stood a large hazel tree. One poem recites that the nuts of this tree fell into the well and were then eaten by the Salmon of Knowledge. In this way the seeds of knowledge were gifted. Drawn to the source of this power, Sinann waded into the waters to retrieve the essence of the knowledge, but she was drowned. This is how Sinann became the goddess associated with the River Shannon. The tale parallels another told of Boand, who also sought knowledge from a Well of Knowledge but was destroyed and became the goddess of the Boyne. *The Metrical Dindshenchas* reveal that *Segais* was the name she was known by in the Otherworld. This suggests that she was actually the goddess of knowledge. Her wisdom comes from *under* the well ie; the Otherworld.[52]

The name of the English Knucker has its origins in the Anglo-Saxon word, *Nicor* – which describes a kind of hybrid sea monster. Knuckers favoured deep pools as their abodes. The Old Icelandic *Nykr* is a fabulous water monster which equates with the old Germanic *Nixie*: a water nymph/sprite. It has also been speculated that there is a connection between the *Nykr* and the Celtic, *Each Uisige* (or Kelpie). Although the latter is a water horse that dwells in rivers and lochs, it does appear to be a manifestation of the same idea: a spirit of the water, or *genus loci*. Accounts of Kelpies range from hideous monsters or alluring female nymphs, but most are regarded as dangerous; luring the unwary to their deaths in troubled waters. The Kelpie itself is described as a horse, often pale in colour with a mane of seaweed. There are images from Pictish art that could be the predecessors for this fabulous creature. Although its mythical and religious roots have been corrupted through time, imagery from Pictish stones paints another picture of a benign beast, sometimes appearing in pairs with their tails entwined. In other images the creature observes scenes from an elevated position, hinting at its importance. However, though not strictly a dragon, the link with water and pools is relevant.[53]

This association sometimes earned serpent-dragons a bad reputation. There was a serpent spring in south of Tripoli, on the Peloponnese peninsula, whose waters thrashed with squirming snakes. A bite from any of them would poison the blood and turn the victim's bones to powder. The origins of this pool were none other than the Medusa herself. Luckily, those who dwelled near the deadly spring were immune to its poison, and were known as the *Psylli*. It was said they possessed some African odour that sent serpents packing and were renowned as great snake-charmers.[54] However, such accounts of wells as negative places is rare (and may account for a shift in religious bias away from serpent/well worship – also hinted at in many of the myths we have examined).

Many tales about wells involved the quest for knowledge, and this insight came with a price, whether it be trial or sacrifice. It's interesting to note that in Norse mythology giants and dragons are sometimes interchangeable. Therefore we have to wonder that when Odin undertakes his ritual journey and is bestowed with the knowledge of the runes by the giant Mimir, whether at one time this giant was also a dragon. Afterall, he dwells within the waters of the well that takes his name: *Mímisbrunnr*.

Overwhelmingly we find that, in the ancient world, wells were where knowledge was sought and where healing was gained – both concepts are associated with the serpent-dragon. The dragon guards the well or it lives in the water. The waters of the spring issue from the earth and are therefore born from the Underworld, or the Earth Goddess herself. However, the snake and the dragon may represent energies emanating from deep within (serpent-dragon energy personified). They were places where oracles were sought, and where they dwelled – here we have the link with sight and vision that appears at the etymological root of 'dragon'. Could it be that the original guardians and spirits of these wells were in fact the serpent-dragons? Many times the *genus loci* (the original spirits of sacred wells and springs) are named as serpents. Is this what the *Drakainas* were too? They are also sometimes called priestesses, which alludes to some organisation and coherent structure to serpent-dragon well worship.

When Apollo arrives at Delphi, he not only slays Python, but Delphyne/Telphusa too. Could such myths reflect a religious upheaval? Dragon slayers killing dragons at wells, who are also sometimes called priestesses. If so this change must have come about long before Christianity – which subsequently appropriated the same imagery for its own purposes.

Rivers also share their store of dragon-lore. Forty Chinese river names contain the word dragon.[55]. In Turkish myth, a subterranean section of the river Orontes was formed when the Islamic Prophet, Khiḍr, chased a dragon there. To flee it burrowed into the earth.[56] The legend is much older than the Islamic one though. The same section of the river is recorded as being known as *Drakon*[57] by a Byzantine chronicler, Ionnes Malalas, writing in the 6th Century CE. And before his work the river was cited by Strabo as being called both Typhon and Ophite:[58] the names of two ancient dragons. Across several provinces of France come stories of the *Drac*. Described variously as a serpent with a human head or a great serpent with a dragon-stone in its forehead, it was seen as a malign and evil being. *Drac* is a shapeshifter, assuming various guises including a horse, and is somewhat reminiscent of the Kelpie. Like a siren it uses song to lure its victims to the River Rhône, where it devours its captives.[59] Macedonia also retained folklore of mean *Drakos* that guarded wells, they sometimes held back the waters.[60]

Staring at the rippling waters of a large river, flowing over stony shallows, the ever-moving surface sometimes forms dozens of arcs, side-by-side, spanning the river like a scaled hide. The fluid animation of the water, coupled with the weaving nature of the river, complete a serpentine illusion. That is not to say this is the reason or origin of these myths. To suggest such a rational explanation isn't the purpose of this book. The link between serpent and water, serpent and spirit/*genus loci,* oracular and healing powers extends far beyond physical origins. Like the waters, it is deeper, and much more profound.

Dragon mythology has endured to this day – shrouded, tamed perhaps, but if we strip away that which is superfluous this myth can reveal something vital about ourselves. Like legend, we all spring from a common root, and although our species has made its way across this earth by different paths, the genetic core remains. Just as with our DNA, so too our myths: the strength of these beliefs is stored within us, even if we don't recognise it. Even if we've had our minds flayed raw by Abrahamic religions, and downplayed by reductionist science, something vital remains in the dragon myth. Something that connects us as a species.

A Gorgon from Corfu

Mothers of Dragons

Dragons are bound in the depths of time. As early as 6000 BC we find clear indications of serpent goddesses and the correlation of the feminine form with serpent imagery. For example, Serbian goddess figurines of this period have been found that wear serpent belts. At a site at Dolnoslav in Bulgaria, dated to the Chalcolithic (4600-4200 BCE), hundreds of snake-headed figures of clay were discovered. From Bronze-Age Mesopotamia, a Babylonian tomb inscription reads: *ama-ushum-gal-anna,* which translates as 'the Mother is the Great Serpent of Heaven'. Vedic texts tell us that the Queen of Snakes was the Earth. She had many names – as Kadru she gave birth to the Nâga race, those magical serpent beings that lived inside the earth or dwelled within the ocean. In the myths of Greece, Mesopotamia and elsewhere the Earth Goddess birthed serpent-dragons.[1]

The serpent-dragons of old are usually entwined with female goddesses, or they are themselves female. Where they are male (such as Zeus Meilichios), these often replaced an earlier serpent deity – possibly a *genus loci* of a well or stream. Sometimes they are gods, like Ningishzida whose sex is wholly ambiguous. This distinction is important. There is a recognisable pattern of masculine and feminine dragons that echoes through the serpent lore. This theme is explored further in a later chapter.[2]

Embedded in Irish lore we hear of a Fomorian Druidess named Dreco. She slew Fergus Lethderg, one of the early Irish settlers who arrived with the leader Nemed (from whom the Nemedians take their name). Dreco is mentioned in the Irish annals as using her knowledge of potions to send the sons of Fergus to sleep, and then dispatching them as they slumbered. The poem that recalls her deed, *Nemthend,* ends in comparing her to a dragon. Although this is likely an inference by the Christian scribe to Satan, her name is of interest and may be a corruption of the Greek: *Drakon,* or *Draco.*[3]

Early Illyrian traditions linked serpent, Moon and female/ goddesses throughout the region. Their *Zmijar* were wizards versed in the secrets of snakes. In Armenia, the wilderness of Mount Massis was home to the 'tribe of the dragon' – shapeshifters that were as comfortable in their human guise as they were that of the serpent. These magicians believed that the great mother, Anush dwelled upon the mountain. She was the mate of Ahi Dahaka.[4]

As we've already discovered, locked within the body of this lore is how the serpent-dragon is linked with water. By such an association, they are thus engaged to the Moon. Such lunar affiliations bring them into the realms of female menstruation and notions of potency, fertility and regeneration: themes governed by the Moon in many cultures. Much goddess worship centres around the silvery disc and its waxing and waning. Sometimes the dragon priestesses' blood is the water itself.

There is also a juxtaposition of the erotic, phallic snake in male form with its feminine associations. The serpent is both. It is sexed and sexless. By its association to water it is bound to the Moon in lunar worship. It is immortal. The dragon transcends and rises to the heavens – but it's also privy to the intimate knowledge of the Underworld in which it dwells.

Serpents are also associated with death and rebirth. In this way they are paired to form a union of symbolism: a complex of triads favoured by the ancients. It's no surprise that dragon and serpent heads commonly appear at the terminals of the three-pronged triskele. This symbol encompassed triadic concepts and was favoured by Celtic and Germanic peoples – as is evidenced in many archaeological finds in these territories.

In Tibet the blue dragon appears in the spring months. It's described as having a long thin neck, a large mouth and long tail. To hear its call of '*ur-ur*' from the broiling cloud was seen as favourable. It appears that balance is also sought here, for the dragon appears when both the winter cold and summer Sun are yet to dominate. The spring is a mix of both, like autumn, it is an intermediary. Could these contrasts, and their unifying quality be part of the symbolism behind the Minoan serpent goddesses? These images of proud women holding serpents in each hand, feature in Pre-Palatial Cretan art. They appear to be the evolution of concepts evidenced in finds across the Aegean from the late Neolithic. Similar imagery appears in other locations far from Crete. Perhaps one of the most north westerly is that found in Ilkley, north Yorkshire. There the snake-bearing figure represents Verbeia, the goddess of the River Wharfe.[5]

In Götland evidence of a serpent cult exists in the many dragonesque carvings scattered across the Baltic island. Some particularly evocative images come from ancient burial sites there, including a famous seated figure who holds two dragon serpents in each hand. Her squatting posture is thought to indicate that she is giving birth, or has given birth to the serpents. It's notable that each of the serpents has a different head and that the artist took pains to distinguish them. The figure comes from Smiss in När Parish and is dated between the 5th and 7th centuries CE. This imagery has been linked by archaeologists to a cult that existed amongst women on the island from the Iron Age and possibly into the 1400s CE.[6]

I'm not suggesting here that these examples, divided as they are by thousands of miles and thousands of years, are evidence of some unified cult. It may be that the serpents represent the spirit of a local river, perhaps even its source or spring. The serpents these figures clasp in their hands might signal the potency of the individual. Or they may be emblematic of the goddess gripping them. But, if so, is she exerting power over them? Or using them to her own ends? The imagery assumes she exerts an element of control, to wield them as objects of power or as wands. Or do these women offer the snakes to those who kneel in veneration before them?

Another idea is that these serpent-dragons, and their related ceremonies/magic, benefitted women. The dragon was its figurehead because it's hunted by men, and only men were dragon slayers.[7] In this case, the dragon, its association with earth goddesses and the Moon, provides a powerful image of feminine worship – something later patriarchal religion despised. Could it be that the medieval inclusion of the maiden, sacrificed to the dragon in Romance stories, isn't a fossil of pagan sacrifice but the remnant of early Christian ideals – driven by a patriarchal need to bury the concept of 'Goddess? That the 'gallant hero' can save the virgin from its clutches is a personification of this male-driven ideal? (In the Far East dragons are overwhelmingly masculine and associated with the Yang principle – chauvinism appears to rear its head here too.)[8]

It's very easy to cast the past in a golden light. But there was no golden age. No doubt many pagans treated their womenfolk as appallingly as the Christians and Muslims. However, patriarchal mores are enshrined in many religious doctrines. When the sky god peers down from his heavenly abode, he follows a pagan trope of a hero no longer willing to work with the mother or her children – instead he is resolutely determined to conquer her, to subdue her.

In some tales women were sometimes accused of having sex with dragons. Although this wasn't considered a sin, their children were inevitably males. The pregnancy drained the mother, leaving her consumptive. They became vehicles for the male progeny who would be blessed with invincibility. Because of this, heroes earned the title 'dragon' – It was usually possible to tell these children from normal humans, for their larger craniums meant that their heads were disproportionate to their bodies. If they took off their shirts then the wings in their armpits would be a sure sign of their heritage. In Slavic folklore, a dragon that wished such a union would appear from the chimney, but we don't hear if the woman had any say in this coupling. Legend tells us that, to get out of such a relationship, the woman had to fumigate herself and then seek out the tree in which the dragon lay. She would place tinder around the trunk and set it alight. No doubt such an endeavour was fraught with danger, and she had to do it before pregnancy occurred.[9]

The hero, Samsar, was birthed by a woman who drank from a magical spring. He subsequently overcame a dragon that controlled the spring – for it supplied water to the city of Sasun. This dragon had hitherto been content with the yearly sacrifice of a girl to placate it.[10] Alexander the Great was also said to have been born of a union between his mother (Olympias) and a serpent.[11]

This association between beast and mother, earth and dragon has given rise to many goddesses whose prodigy are often dragons. Their lineage is long. There are refrains of such a being in the personage of Baba-Yaga. As Queen of Dragons she controls the many-headed Chudo-Yudo, who waits by the sacred well, wherein lie the waters of Life and Death. Some say this dragon is actually her brother. Then there is Kosh-Chei the Deathless, a dragon in human guise, an immortal who was given a soul by Baba-Yaga. She also makes an appearance in the tale of Princess Vasilissa, who was kidnapped by a powerful dragon that dwelled within a golden castle that sat atop a silver pillar. Her brothers tried to save her but failed and were imprisoned alongside their sister in the dragon's lair. Their heartbroken mother swallowed a magical pea that grew inside her, until she conceived a divine son, named Ivan the Pea. He grew strong and matured quickly. Heading out to save his kin, Ivan came across a revolving hut set on giant chicken legs. Baba Yaga appeared to the youth in the guise of an old crone. She gave him direction and asked for the magic water that the dragon guarded, for it would restore her youth. Ivan employed a blacksmith to forge him a great mace, so big fifty men could barely shoulder it. He used this weapon when he confronted the dragon, smashing it to bits and freeing the princess. He then fulfilled his promise to Baba Yaga.

Here again we have the echo of an ancient refrain: that of the crone goddess and the waters of Life and Death guarded by a dragon (the one in this tale has a human body and dragon-head, and flies upon the back of a winged black horse). Ivan is a strong-man like Thor or Perun, whose mace replaces the hammer, *mjolnir*. Ivan's conception, and rapid aging, from babe to youth are reminiscent of other divine youths, such as Oengus mac Óg.

Most often portrayed as a toothless hag, Baby Yaga was most likely once a goddess in antiquity. Although she was supposed to spin the thread of fate with the entrails of the dead, she was also a healer. She may have been associated with the well-being of herds and horses. In folklore she dwells deep in the woods, roving around in a little hut that walks on giant chicken legs. In some accounts there is something of the gorgon about her, for her locks are a mass of writhing snakes. But she can also appear like a gentle old lady, with a kindly nature. It stands to reason that she is a triple goddess, with a nod to the ancient fates of antiquity. In this respect she appears to bear a resemblance to both Valkyrie and Nornir of the Scandinavian diaspora. Indeed she is likened to *Volkhvy*, who resemble the wise old volva of Norse myth. These were wise women, seers and healers, once highly respected in their cultures before the advent of Christianity.[12]

Like Baba Yaga, the Greek Gorgon might be a goddess in her own right. Imagery in which she is flanked by lions or other animals offer us an glimpse of a 'mistress of beasts' (and possibly a nod to Artemis the Huntress). In an image from Cofu, a huge gorgon grips two serpents and her belt is formed by another knotted around her waist. Another image from Palaikastro (Crete) depicts her in a similar aspect. In Asia Minor, she is associated with Cybele and her glaring image appears on Zeus' shield, known as the *Aegis*. She is likely linked with lunar cycles and magical rites. Clement of Alexandria noted that the Orphic cult called the Moon *Gorgoneion.*[13]

Other legends tell of three gorgons who dwell at the end of the earth, in a realm of darkness and cloud. Medusa is one of them. They are surrounded by statues – the petrified victims of her terrible glare. It was said that Medusa's blood yielded two distinct potions – one that ushered in death, another that could restore life. Asclepius was gifted these potions by Athena, but suffered the wrath of Zeus when he brought the dead back to life.[14]

Like the Gorgon, the Lamia is a mysterious and much maligned character. It is strange that Apollo, who slew the great serpent at Delphi, declined to do the same to Sybaris – a Lamia that dwelled across the valley from Delphi, in the Cave of Kirphis. Sybaris is described as a giant beast that crawled forth each day to kidnap children and devour local herds. When Apollo's worshippers beseeched the god to do something about the monster, Apollo suggested the sacrifice of a Delphian boy, Alkyoneus. Fortunately the youth was saved by an Aetolian hero, Eurybatos – for the hero fell in love with Alkyoneus and took himself to Sybaris' cave, where he confronted the monster, dragging her out and tossing her over a precipice. In the spot where she fell a spring of water gushed from the ground. The spring was named after the monster.[15]

Skylla, a sea monster, was the daughter of a Lamia – named as being either Echidna (who birthed many a monster) or Hekate. *Laminae* also appear in later folklore; variously as vampiric seductresses, draining mortal men of their very essence, or snatching babies and sometimes even eating them. Referred to as demons, they are commonly depicted as half-serpent females and are similar in form to the Nâga. The most famous Lamia was a queen from ancient Libya. Zeus fawned over her and thus she incurred the wrath of Hera. From that point on the queen's life took a terrible turn. Every child she bore died and with each death part of her spirit became embittered. As her nature changed so too jealously gripped her heart. She roved the land, stealing the children of others and, because she was so hateful, ripping them to shreds. Some say that she even ate the remains. Like an animal, this Lamia dwelled in a cave, but there was no refuge from the ugliness that filled her. Even sleep was no option – for Hera also cursed her with insomnia. Zeus pitied what she'd become (perhaps aware that his many sexual ventures left a bitter taste in Hera's mouth). Thus he allowed the Lamia the ability to take out her eyes and keep them in a box. This way she could find some respite in sleep.[16]

Another Lamia appears in the form of *Poena*. She sought to avenge the death of one of Apollo's lovers, Psamathe, who was buried alive by her father. Raging against the townsfolk of Argos, this creature was described as half-serpent with Medusa-like hair. She attacked mothers, wrenched their children from them and devoured them whole. A young hero of the town, Koroibos, rose up to repel the beast. Aided by his band of warriors, he slew the Lamia – but this only stoked the fires of Apollo's wrath and the god sent a plague upon the town. The Lamia had other guises too and was identified with the cannibalistic child-stealing entities, Mormo, Gello, Karko and Empusa – phantasms that performed Hekate's bidding and sometimes appeared to be aspects of the goddess – she is even sometimes called by these names. As her minions they are known as the *Hekataia*. They were androgynous, or contain masculine and feminine elements.[17]

Intriguingly there's a Lithuanian goddess of fate named Laima (also Lauma) who sits upon a hill, before a silver altar (perhaps a kenning for a well?). She had a role in the protection of children – a far cry from the negative connotations of the Lamia. On a deeper level she is involved in the relationship of events and their place in Time. She addresses the worth of a life, giving reward or punishment as due. Laima forms a triad alongside Gegutė – the cuckoo goddess, who is intimate with cyclical time and bears responsibly for it – and Perkunas, who carries out the judgements of Laima.[18]

Here too we possibly have a link with another set of goddesses, who might at first seem to bear little that is dragon-like about them. Both the Grecian *Morai* and the Scandinavian *Nornir* form triads of fate controlling goddesses. They are also all closely associated with wells. The Nornir's well lays at the foot of the great world tree, *Yggdrasil*, whose roots are chewed upon by *Nidhoggr*. In the *Laminae* there are hints at the same kind of treatment that the so-called dragonesses, Delphyne and Telphusa, endured at the hands of Apollo. The notion of the dragon-well is already well attested in Greece, as is that of the *drakaina* – female dragon. The Lamia appear to form part of this corpus, and hint at a cultic shift – perhaps a denigration of the Earth Goddess cult of Ge (or Gaia) at Delphi, echoed in the tales of Sybaris and *Poena.*[19]

There also exists a mythological precedent for the link between time and the serpent in its cosmic form. In ancient Egypt Time itself is likened to an endless serpent. In the North, the *Nornir* situate themselves at a well and, from this vantage point, look down the serpentine flow of the waters of time, with its surface rippling like scales. It is an endless cycle of time: the river flows to the ocean, clouds form, rains come, feeding the river that again feeds the ocean. Fate was a complex concept in the pagan sphere. Many sought auguries and diviners to glimpse what might come to pass. Yet what was glimpsed was believed to be unavoidable. If an event was fated to occur, nothing that person did could halt it. In fact their trying to avoid something often steered them toward it.

Perhaps one of the most intriguing of the dragon hybrids is that of the Nâga and their ilk. Having the upper bodies of humans and the lower of serpents, they appear to bridge the gap between the monstrous and the human. Their form echoes that of the Laminae and other Grecian characters such as Cecrops. They could also appear in serpent form or as multi-headed cobras, which were known as *Sapta-Nâgas*. They were believed to be divine and there were seven of these Sapta-Nâgas: Takshâka, Karka, Padma, Mahapâdma, Sank-haka, Gulike and Ananta.[20] Both divine and lesser Nâga conform (almost with precision) to what we've previously learned about dragons.

Although their description is similar to the Laminae, they didn't invoke the same sense of dread. Nâga kept knowledge and they were teachers of magical arts and occult sciences. There are many tales of Nâga kings who guarded great treasures. The females of their kind were called *Nâgī*, the males *Nâga*.[21] Much myth surrounding them is connected with water and the underworld, and they were viewed as primordial beings whose creators were Kas'yâpa-pra-jâpati and Kadrû (by another telling, Manasa Devi was the mother of all Nâgas).[22]

Sesha was a Nâga king who ruled the underworld of Pātāla. He was sometimes visualised wearing purple robes and holding aloft a pestle and plough. Sesha also possessed a cosmic nature and was an allegory of time eternal. To the Hindus, as to pagan peoples in general, time was not a sequence of moments from point Alpha to Omega. Instead it followed the intuitive notion of a series of cycles. At the end of a span of 1,000 ages (*Kalpa*) Sesha destroys the world: a purification like a wild-fire through a forest, making way for new growth.[23] Numerous myths the world over tell us of these cycles: the raising and destruction of civilisations by the gods. Sesha's name means 'eternal' and he was also known as Ananta.

The knowledge of the Nâga was too powerful for humans, and some tales warned against them. It was said that, because they'd absorbed poison from the waters of creation, they could be harmful. Still, some humans travelled to their worlds,[24] and some Nâga even fell in love with human women. The offspring of such unions would be demi-gods. Unsurprisingly, royal lineages sought to trace their ancestry to this mysterious race of godly beings. It also accounts for the fact that some Nâga refer to actual personages from history, such as Takeshaka.

It was told that the Nâga possessed a sacred jewel that was stored in the back of their throats. Should they cough it up, the gemstone would shine like the sun, illuminating all.[25] This magical artefact reads like a metaphor for the illuminating wisdom of their race being transmitted by spoken word.

The land of the Nâga was named *Nâgaloka* and it was filled with beautiful palaces and temples. With its own geography and lore, the land of the Nâga functioned like an unearthly paradise. *Bhogavati*, 'the Town of Serpents', was where pleasure was the rule and *Pātāla* was its most famed palace. *Nâgaloka*, was divided into levels, the lowest being where *Pātāla* was located – but this wasn't like some Christian descent into the depths of Hell, for the deeper realms were even more wondrous than those above. Here, even the Nâga were adorned in bright gemstones. Often the doorway to this realm was located in an anthill, other times in caves.[26]

It was told that one tribe of Nâga lived within the ocean, another within the mountains and occasionally there was rivalry between the two. But there were also Nâga who dwelled in the heavenly palaces and divine Nâga which caused clouds to rise and rain to fall. Earthly Nâga worked beneficially with waterways, and hidden Nâga guarded treasure. Conforming to their brethren, many Nâga are associated with rivers, pools and lakes. In such locations they fulfil the role of serpent guardian/ spirit or *genus loci*. As we've seen, this belief is very widespread indeed, and very ancient.[27]

Carved images of them were also often kept beneath sacred fig trees, banyan and pipal trees. These carved stones, known as *nāgakals*, can be found sited beneath sacred trees or village ponds. They appear to have symbolised some fertility aspect and were visited by women desiring children. Upon completing a *nāgakal* the sculptor immersed the stone in the pond to imbue it with the power of the waters – it could remain submerged for up to six months.[28]

In Kashmir the word *Nag* appears in regards to many reservoirs, springs and rivers. Nâga worship was prolific in this region and was seen as a branch of Hinduism and a folk religion. It's recorded that there were some six-hundred Nâga who were worshipped in the province, often in mountain passes. It was even said that at one time Kashmir was ruled by Ananta/Sesha. In the time of Alexander the Great, cultists in Kashmir mountains kept giant snakes in caves and revered them. An attempt to convert the inhabitants of the mountain valleys to Buddhism was repulsed by Nâga worshippers in the 3rd or 4th centuries BCE. However, as Buddhism persisted, the Nâga religion declined. By the 11th century CE it was gone. Hinduism was more sympathetic to the Nâga cults and didn't seek to eradicate them.[29]

This relationship between Buddhist and Nâga cult is interesting. It was said the Dali Lama gave Nâga teachings. The Buddha himself was reputed to have become one in a previous incarnation because he wished to understand their occult wisdom. Another story even implies that the Buddha, realising that the full breadth of his vision was too much for humanity in its current state, gathered the Nâga and revealed to them his deeper understanding of the universal void. Thus, to his human followers, he only revealed a simpler version of his teachings. Several centuries later the sage, Nāgārjuna was initiated by the serpent kings about the truth of the void (*Śūnya*) which he could then reveal to the people.[30]

Whatever the truth of this, some form of Nâga teaching was incorporated into the new religion. By 1056 CE Buddhist texts had been altered to accommodate what was a popular folk religion, incorporating the Nâga into their corpus. Indeed the famous tale is told about the Nâga king, Muchilinda, who protected the Buddha as he mediated beneath the Bodhi tree on the shores of Lake Muchilinda. A storm raged for seven days and seven nights and Muchilinda coiled around him seven times. This picture of unity is somewhat offset by numerous stories that relate how the Buddha triumphed over different Nâga, and in this context they're usually billed as malicious serpents.[31]

Here, once again, we have evidence of a trend of religious upheaval, the denigration of serpent lore and appropriation of its imagery. Previously Nâga worship was prolific and wasn't only confined to the Kashmir region. They appear in Nepal, Thailand, Cambodia, Malaysia, India, Japan and China. In Burma, initiation ceremonies and Nâga statues existed until recently. The Burmese Nâga bore a lot in common with the dragon of Chinese and Indian lore. There are even tales that Nâga workmen laboured on ancient temples, and their youths attended the courts of kings.[32]

Could it be that another Indian fire-breathing monster, known as Makara reflects a certain religious schism. Makara is the mount of both Varuna – styled as the master of the cosmic waters – and Ganga, the eponymous river goddess of the Ganges (whose waters flow through the three realms of heavens, our reality and the underworld). Could the imagery reflect the domination of Varuna over earlier animist cults? The image of a dragon as a mount or steed is one that also appears on many cylinder seals from ancient Mesopotamia. Makara presides over the Waters of Life and Death. Echoing its Japanese counterparts, he carries a pearl in his mouth. This gem brings true love to whoever is brave enough to snatch it from monster's jaws. Makara underwent something of a metamorphic shift through the ages, and is also portrayed as a dolphin, crab and fish-elephant. However, his oldest form is that of a crocodile. In Java, Makara is a noun used for a type of sea-monster with close associations to darkness and water. Its symbol was also used by the Mara, a tribe that rose to attack the Buddha.[33]

Interestingly, Nâga imagery was used in pre-Hindu Tantra, in which the masculine was Shiva (*Nâga*) and the feminine Shakti, (*Nâgi*).[34] Here the roles are defined in a very symbolic way. This duality can be traced in much serpent-dragon worship elsewhere.

How far back do such concepts extend? The ancient Harappan culture flourished in the Indus valley around the third millennium BCE. Imagery of the period portrays worshippers with cobras rising behind them. The sacred pipal tree also makes an appearance, and one seal even depicts a cobra seated upon a throne beneath such a tree.[35]

In Arabic culture the Nâga-serpent appears in the form of the Jinn. Not the turbaned cliche popularised by Disney, but in their true form they are much more subtle. As serpents, Jinn inhabited sources of water. They were even recognised in the Qur'ān, albeit with a measure of distain. They were believed to be the spirts of trees, at home in the moistness of their roots. They also liked to dwell in caves, at springs and wells. Jinn were invisible but could choose to manifest themselves as amphibians and snakes. They were taken to be semi-divine. Being one of the most prolific and sacred effigies of the numerous pagan cults in Islamic territory, it is little wonder that Mohammed dealt with the serpent so ruthlessly. The practices did not yield overnight even though Mohammed gave orders to destroy them.[36]

Whether it be Buddhism, Zoroastrianism, Islam or Christianity, all sought to put down an older belief system. This belief appears to revolve around ancient goddess and animist worship. Embodied in the corpus of this lore was the veneration of the Earth in mother form, the World Tree and Well. At such places healing and oracles were sought. Some of these places were attended by priestesses. Here the *genus loci,* the animist spirit of the locale, was propitiated with libation and sacrifice. These spirits were believed to be serpent-dragons – the original dragon is thus revealed.

The Immortal Healer

Just as we begin to soar into the heady realms of cosmic creation, we return to the material world. For although associated with such lofty ideals, the dragon and its parallel, the serpent, were woven into the very fabric of ordinary life. We have seen how people revered the serpent of hearth and home, but so too, they were powers that healed. Their association with wells confirms this. And, just as the dragon is irrefutably linked with waters, it is also associated with healing. Not only because the serpent sheds its skin and is reborn, or because its venom is also a powerful antidote – these natural phenomena collude with the healing nature of water itself. The identification of water as the life-giving principle binds it to the mythos of the dragon.

A curious piece of folklore comes from Sutherland in Scotland. In this tale Farquhar the drover comes across a doctor who enquires about his hazel staff. Revealing that he took it from Glen Gollig, the doctor requests that Farquhar get him one too. It's obvious that the doctor knows of the spot, because he adds that Farquhar is to look for a hole at the base of the hazel. Six serpents will appear from beneath the tree, and Farquhar must place a bottle over the entrance to capture the seventh. This magical creature is the fabled White Adder. The drover does as he's bid and returns to the doctor. They make a stew from the serpent, but Farquhar burns his finger while stirring the broth. Scalded he puts thumb to mouth and receives great knowledge, but says nothing. When the doctor takes a sip he quickly realises that the essence is gone from the broth.

As Farquhar the healer (*leigheach*) he becomes a travelling doctor, and there's no ailment he cannot cure. Eventually he arrives at the palace of the King and shouts "*An daol dubh ris a chnamh gheal*" (the black beetle to the white bone). For three days he goes there each morning and hollers this cryptic verse. The king, suffering from great pain in his knee, hears Farquhar's cry and bids his guards bring the healer to him. Farquhar quickly reveals that the king's own doctors have been prolonging his distress to fuel their coffers, by placing a black beetle in the king's wound![1]

A similar story tells of the three Beaton brothers from Islay. They were all healers, though Gilleadha was most famous, for he'd also captured a white adder and made a broth of it. Accidentally partaking of this broth, he gained profound insight into his profession, so that he was the favoured herbalist of the Scottish king.[2]

These tales have a precedent in an older legend involving Fionn mac Cumhail, which relates how the youth was commanded to catch the Salmon of Knowledge. In the Scots version he is commanded by giants, while in the Irish tale it's a Druid. Either way, while cooking the fish the hero burns his thumb and sticks it in his mouth, gaining the potent insight for himself. The pattern is very similar, but of a much earlier age. The lore had a long pedigree and even into the mid-1800s serpents were associated with healing in the Highlands.[3]

The Brother's Grimm collected many European folktales. Amongst them, the *Legend of the White Snake* tells of a king bestowed with magical powers. Every evening a covered plate of food was brought to him, but no one was allowed to see what was on the dish. One day an inquisitive servant took a peek and saw it was a boiled white snake. Trying a portion the servant suddenly understood the chatter of both birds and the animals. This skill came in handy when the queen lost her ring and blamed this same servant, for he overheard two ducks chatting and one admitted to swallowing the ring. He swiftly grabbed the duck and dragged it to the cook. After being nicely roasted it was cut open to reveal the ring inside and the servant saved himself from the dungeons. As a reward he was granted his wish of owning a horse provisioned for a journey – for the servant's chief desire was to see the world. He hadn't gone far upon his journey before he'd saved three beached fishes, listened to the ant-king's complaints about the servant's clumsy horse (which he then slaughtered to placate the tiny king) and saved the fledglings of ravens that had been tossed from their nests. Each of these creatures would subsequently come to his aid as he tried to win the hand of a princess. Because of his lowly status she'd put him to task. So the fish retrieved a ring tossed to the waves, the ant-king sent his minions to collect grain and the ravens fetched a golden apple from the Tree of Life (only upon sharing the apple with the servant does the heart of the princess open up).[4]

Although healing isn't a feature, the servant understands the language of the birds, just like Sigurd in the *Volsung Saga*. The Tree of Life, with its golden apples, also makes an appearance. The tale holds within it familiar seeds, germinated from older mythology. Hinting at both Celtic and Norse motifs, it is thoroughly Germanic in nature.

As we've seen, the ancient Greeks held the snake in great esteem for its healing affinities. The *Asclepions* of the healing god are a fine example of this practice.[5] We've also now seen that the snake's beneficial powers were still remembered in folklore of the 1800s, in both Celtic and Germanic lands, themselves vested with lingering refrains of older myths, like a nod to the serpent lore of old.

It appears that with the establishment of the Church in the West, the serpent suffered under the stigma of its devilish association. The 7th century CE text known as the *Lacnunga Manuscript* hails from Anglo-Saxon England. Although containing elements of paganism, it appears to reflect the Christian bias against the snake. It contains the 'Nine Herb Charm' which recounts that dragons, serpents and worms were all said to cause illness – there were nine serpents that caused the nine main illnesses.

We can't only blame the Christians for disliking the serpent. There seems to be a thread of distain toward snakes and dragons running through Norse and Germanic legends. Thor is poisoned by Jörmungandr's poison, and Beowulf is overcome by the venomous bite of a dragon. Many dragons and worms had poisonous breath or blood and they were associated with disease and plague. A tale from the Welsh *Mabinogion*, named 'Lludd and Llefelys,' recounts how these two brothers were involved in kingship struggles for the kingdom of Britain.[6] However, their lands were beset by three plagues. The second of these occurred every May Day, when a terrible scream issued across the land. This sound was so harrowing that pregnant women lost their children, and all living things became barren. Discovering the source of this plague revealed two dragons locked in combat: a red dragon battled a white one. To remedy their curse both were sealed within a stone chest and buried in the centre of the kingdom. This tale parallels the early Arthurian tale in which Merlin (Ambrosius) reveals two dragons that are contained in vases, hidden within an underground pool beneath the castle of king Vortigern.[7]

At the beginning of 793 CE the *Anglo Saxon Chronicle* reported that a fiery dragon was sighted in the skies above England – this portent ushered in great famine, and on the 8th of January a Viking raiding party shocked Christendom when it attacked Lindisfarne. It was a harbinger of things to come. This notion of dragons being portents of plague wasn't confined to the Saxons. Another Christian report, from the Lombardic historian Paul the Deacon, tells of how the waters of the Tiber rose, flooding Rome.[8] A great many serpents and even a great dragon were seen floating in the river. A terrible pestilence followed – realistically, after such an inundation, the drinking supply within the city would have been contaminated: perfect conditions for disease to run rife.

In the Philosophy known as 'The Doctrine of Signatures', the form of a natural object reflects its use. Thus snake-like or dragon-like plants might aid against the poison of a serpent – or at least deter them from striking. Variations of *Arum Dracuticulus* are known as the 'flower of the Dragon'. Its lurid purple flower resembles a tongue or viper's head, (the effect enhanced by its speckled hue and thick purple stamen). It has a carrion smell and was said to protect against snakes. The herbalist Gerard suggested they were also effective against pestilence and poison. There are other dragon plants, such as tarragon (called *dragoncello* in Italy) and *dracontium*, which was also believed to relieve the poison given by snakebites.[9]

And here we return, like the ouroboros biting its tail, to the earliest written myths. In the epic of Gilgamesh, committed to clay tablets at the dawn of civilisation, the hero retrieves the sacred herb of immortality from the bottom of the ocean. However, as he rests, a snake creeps from a deep pool and snatches the herb, sloughing off its skin to return into the waters – renewed, the immortal serpent is reborn.

Chapter 4

The Alchemy of Dragons

The Serpent That Encircles the World

Ouroboros from the Codex Marcianus

We have come far. Whisking across the continents in search of ancient beasts and their origins, legends and lore. We take some respite and well-earned rest in our great library, amongst the hallowed tomes. Opening up a great alchemical text we stare in amazement. On the pages spread before us we see images of winged dragons perched atop alchemical containers, their funnels spewing sulphurous gases to the heavens. In pairs, dragons circle each other, framing strange scenes that are realistic views of laboratories and implements, themselves decorated with strange symbols: winding serpents and astrological emblems. We are familiar with some of these tools, for they line the shelves and tables of our own alchemical lair. These are the hermetic texts of the 1600s and 1700s. They owe their influence to a much older tradition. As we shall uncover, the dragon also plays a vital role here.

In the following pages I wish to uncover the evidence that points to the profundity of their imagery, and the concepts buried behind them. We shall discover knowledge that draws from some of the oldest mythology on the planet. We shall also stray into the world of abstracts and concepts. Here symbol and image collide to form powerful *dragonesque* entities. Prepare to dive deep into the pool of the dragon.

In medieval alchemy the dragon is a mercurial creature and a symbol of transformation. Drawing on more ancient ideas, medieval alchemy retained many of its earlier 'pagan' qualities. The adoption of the ouroboros is a case in point.

Ancient cartographers drew maps of their world with their own countries at the centre: This civilised hub was invariably surrounded by barbarians, and all the lands were girded by an ocean, itself encircled by the World Serpent, gripping its tail in its mouth. Egyptians, Greeks and Norse all possessed the myth of the primordial serpent that surrounded the ocean. So too, in the Middle Ages, cartographers bounded the earth with the Zodiacal Serpent, upon whose scales astrological signs were inscribed. Beyond this ouroboros lay the cosmic waters, or chaotic abyss.

This speaks to the strength and sustainability of such a symbol. The testimony of the dragon's symbolic endurance is its adaptation into alchemical and hermetic lore as the ouroboros. There's an almost a subconscious symbolism here: the idea of the World Serpent as a frontier to the unknown. It delineates the boundary of the material world from the immaterial, creation from extinction. The Egyptians called it Sito, the Norse Jörmungandr. Over great spans of time and distance it is the same.

Sito, Son of the Earth, is the Egyptian ouroboros. It was supposed to have surrounded the sacred city of Hermopolis, but he also girded the known world, protecting it from the surrounding ocean/primal waters. In effect Sito was the line between the manifest world and the waters of the cosmos. In the *Book of the Dead* it's revealed that Sito dies and is then reborn each day. This suggests that he undertakes a journey to the underworld, like Rě upon the solar barge. Sito is ancient and everlasting. According to the *Coffin Texts*, the divine creative entity that uttered the first word was this serpent, encircled by its own coils. It transformed into the supreme god, Ptah, but will one day return to its serpent form. The ouroboros and a paired serpent of sky and earth appear on Egyptian Funerary coffins, such as that on the shrine of Tutankhamun.[1]

The earliest depiction of the ouroboros dates from 4500 BCE; an image from China dated to the time of the Yang-shao culture, and Susa, in the Near East, dated at 3000 BCE. It's also found amongst the Jaina religion and some tantric cults, where the symbol is associated with the dual principle of ascending (*utsarpinī*) and descending (*avasarpinī*).[2]

It also appears as a motif representing the earliest concept of time in the pagan world. Ouroboros means tail-biter. The medieval alchemical dragon is usually depicted as winged, with a bird-like head. In this context it represented the universal world spirit. Shorn of wings, this loftiness is curtailed and the dragon remains upon the earth: bound to it and therefore earth's representative. Sometimes the two serpents appear in one symbol, but their significance remains the same: change and the cycle of the year, sloughing off the skin of old time to be renewed, and the unity of matter with spirit (alchemical serpent imagery also included coiled serpents, forming loops or rings, numbering between two and four. They were specifically coloured, red or green; indicative of various chemical processes and elements).[3]

The symbol featured in magical and gnostic circles. Hellenistic astrologers assigned the ouroboros to the ninth sphere of the heavens, and this idea possibly had origins in the earlier Babylonian mythology of the celestial serpent. The ouroboros also makes an appearance in the *Acts of Thomas* as the world-girding, tail-chomping serpent – which is likened to Leviathan by many.[4]

In the Gnostic text, *Pistis Sophia,* dragon imagery is both positive and negative, for it is the encircling darkness of ignorance. Within it are located twelve hellish chambers, to which the souls of unrepentant sinners are consigned. These realms are ruled by demonic overlords, and the Dragon of Darkness, with tail in mouth, seals them inside like a sinister lock. The text states that to know the mystery of one of the twelve names of the Dragon of Outer Darkness, will free the imprisoned – affording them a chance of redemption. There are twelve names, but to know one is to know all. The torments of these cycles are apparently contained within the belly of this dragon. In the form of an ouroboros the dragon also appears in the sun, while two dragons steer the bull-driven boat of the Moon. Here we seem to have a somewhat garbled fusion of oriental and Christian themes. It could also indicate that people sought an escape from the pre-Christian concept of endlessness and the eternal return. The keys from the dungeon of this tough material world were to be revealed through the illumination and discovery of these names.[5]

It's been pointed out that the ouroboros in the Sun hints at a more balanced origin for the *Pistis Sophia* – in which there might have been both a Dragon of Darkness and a Dragon of Light. This would make sense, as many of these ideas were filtering through from the East. The Dragon of Darkness may be a corruption of the concept of the cosmic waters. There are also ancient Egyptian ideas at play within *Pistis Sophia.* One suggestion is that the text is the work of Barbelo-Gnostics, a sect based in Syria – although the original text is *Sahidic,* which is a Coptic dialect. It might also be that the Dragon of Light originates from Neoplatonist sources.[6]

The adoption of the serpent as a symbol of time was not new. The Egyptians' use of a cosmic serpent was their way of envisioning the endless flow of time (mentioned as early as 2350 BCE). It became known as Aeon to the gnostics and was also incorporated into the imagery of Aion, in which the Serpent of Time winds around a lion-faced deity. It's said that in the Duat, the Egyptian halls of the dead, the god Khepri is attended by a protective serpent that coils around his body. It has a varying number of heads and places its tail in its mouth. The imagery is strikingly similar to Aion.[7]

The ouroboros as a principle of wholeness and oneness can be traced to pre-Socratic philosophers such as Xenophanes of Colophon (570-460BCE) and Theophrastus of Eresos (sometime in 400 BCE). These thinkers postulated that behind the variety of the 'many things' lay one uniting principle. The 'One is the All,' runs the formula which accompanies a pictorial representation of the ouroboros on the *Leyden Papyri* (dated to between 250-230 CE). An Orphic verse preserved by Clement of Alexandria is: "All things are one in which all these things revolve: fire and water and earth". It came to embrace many cyclic systems as it is unending and so encompassed time and the cycles of birth, death and rebirth.[8]

The Ouroboros is also found in the *Codex Marcianus* which is dated to the 2nd century CE. With its distinctive black and white imagery it is very evocative of the Chinese *yin yang* emblem. Indeed the system of opposites permeate alchemical systems in both the East and the West.

The contradictory pair of dragon and tiger were adopted in Chinese alchemy, and were used to signify various ingredients or equipment, such as tripod and furnace. The pairing is nuanced and poetic. The dragon-tiger becomes malleable and hints at the Taoist way of the ten thousand things. The dragon soars above, mingling with the cloud, eyed by the tiger, grounded on the earth below. This symbology precedes that of *yin yang* and is exceedingly old. Here, the dragon expresses the principle of *yang*. It is the black dragon that turns *yin* into light.[9]

It's important to remember that the introduction of the serpent imagery into western alchemy; alongside gnostic and hermetic thought, was the result of many different schools stemming back to the Orphic mystery cults. The *Prima Materia* was the name given for the source from which everything comes (although Greek philosophers argued over its composition).[10]

Western alchemy also used the pairing of opposites in many of its formulae. Functioning on an ordinary level, these experiments also possessed spiritual significance. These processes were believed to be applicable as much to the salvation of the soul as they were to altering material. The theory of cosmic correspondence is that the outer reflects the inner, the macrocosm the microcosm. Thus the planets were held to directly influence material, and therefore the outcome of results. This also applies to sympathetic magic. Such concepts are apparently of oriental origin.[11]

The idea of one world and one soul, one pervading *pneuma* that permeated the universe can also be traced in the East and the West, for it is similar to Taoist concepts of oneness. Even the Abrahamic belief systems taught that *pneuma*, which they named after tribal sky gods, was in everything and was the cause of all things. For example, in the Koran, Allah is in everything at all times. This concept is what later writers have called the Perennial Philosophy. This is the main-frame of many belief systems and a concept, which, as we can see, is essentially the same. I have already noted in an earlier chapter that some ancient philosophers believed *pneuma* was like a serpent.[12]

Orphism

In Orphic tradition creation was viewed as a series of metaphoric events, grouped into triads. In the version forwarded by the ancient scholars, Hieronymus and Hellanicus, water and matter were the first principles, but these are surrounded by a third principle named *dragon*. Of course, such teachings influenced later gnostic texts. In many respects this principle may well have provided the origin for the *Pistis Sophia's* claim that the Dragon of Darkness surrounded matter. Here, the dragon was a symbol of a vital process. It was imagined as having three heads, those of a bull and lion, and with the central face being the god itself. Wings sprouted from the creature's shoulders adding to its dragon-like appearance. It was said that this being contained within it both masculine and feminine and was the generative cause of all things.[1]

The origins of this sect lay in the fortunes of Orpheus – the itinerant bard said to come from northern climes. Legend tells us that Orpheus was slain by one of Zeus' thunderbolts. However, his decapitated head floated to Lesbos, still singing away to itself. This divine device was kept within a temple of Dionysus, where it still went on prophesying and singing. He later became the prophet of the Orphites.[2]

His followers held that the body was an illusionary image of the immortal soul. The soul was viewed as a fallen *daimon*, that sometimes remembered itself, other times forgot. It passed through endless cycles of life, death and rebirth, becoming lost in them – but by remembrance and contemplation, it could be recollected (*anamnesis*). The ultimate goal was for the divine soul/*daimon*, to rejoin the gods. Initiates to the sect were known as *Bakchoi*. Through various rites, such as the *Dionysis Bakchois*, initiates sought a maddened state, while the *Dionysis Lusios* freed them from this madness. Another rite, the *Lusioi Teletai*, was a purification ceremony. They also performed *Pharmaka* (healing charms) and the incantations of *Epodai*.[3]

Like Pythagoreanism, reality could be expressed by number, geometry and harmony. This shifted the emphasis from what awaited the soul in Hades and inferred an interior, transcendental life in the Now. By embracing cultic rituals – which included the process of recollection and the contemplation of orphic principles – they attempted to gain an awareness of one's eternal soul; its past-lives and deaths, all with the goal of release from these cycles. Stripped of its cultic trapping, this is similar to Buddhist concepts and those of the Upanishads, in which the soul is all (Atman), seeking to be released from the cycle of endless return. Like Eastern concepts of Yoga, adepts sought to yoke themselves by awareness of their inner soul. Pythagoreanism and Orphism share common roots that run parallel to each other in many aspects (such as their adherence to vegetarianism). Several Orphic hymns were attributed to the hand of Pythagoras.[4]

The Hellenised Jews of the 2nd Century BCE said that Orpheus learned all he knew from Moses: a way of subordinating the Orphic creed. They also claimed that all Greek myth came from the Pentateuch. More realistically there are definite links between Dionysian rites and Orphism. The latter utilised Dionysian ecstatic techniques in their practices. They also practiced divination from animal entrails and astrology. Orphism was influential in the 6th Century BCE. Taking elements of earlier cultures, it melded Akkadian and Hittite ideas with Egyptian metaphysics. The Harrans of Ancient Syria said that Orpheus was their religion's founder, and also called him Agathodaimon. Their ceremonies included ritual dismemberment and rebirth, echoing the fate of Orpheus himself.[5]

Connected to the Orphic sect is the intriguing myth of the Orphic egg. Though a number of creation myths have been preserved from ancient Greece, some featured in the mystery cult, and were a mix of myth, magic and metaphor. Eurynome danced upon the waters of the cosmic ocean and kneaded the breeze between her fingers until it became the great serpent, Ophion, which proceeded to curl around her affectionately. It impregnated her and she turned into a dove who lay a single cosmic egg that floated upon the waters. To keep the egg safe, Ophion curled about it seven times until it split in two. From the egg all the things in the world were released. However, Ophion and Eurynome disagreed over who was responsible for creation, they argued and she banished him to a cave deep within the earth.[6]

Epicurus says that the world began as the cosmic egg, around which Time (Kronos) and Inevitability (Ananke) wound like serpents, they squeezed the egg until it separated into Heaven (Ouranos) and Earth (Gaia). The Egyptians told a similar primeval myth, in which the egg of creation rested upon the waters of chaos. The hermaphrodite god, Atum, appeared in serpent-form and cracked it open as he wound about it (in another version the Cosmic Goose performs this deed).[7]

With echoes of the Egyptian mythos from the lands surrounding the sacred city of Hermopolis (with its sacred Ogdoad of masculine and feminine pairs) is a very old myth from Mali: their god, Mangala, created a cosmic egg that became divided into two 'seeds,' so that it could procreate. This gave rise to another six seeds.[8]

It would be tempting to suggest that these myths originate with the Indo-European peoples, but then that doesn't explain its appearance in cultures that are not considered to be part of their expansion. For example, in Fiji the giant serpent Degei always existed. It lived in the sky with a female hawk called Turukawa. Through their union the bird lay two eggs, one containing the proto-man, the other proto-woman. Degei circled around the eggs and when they hatched it created the bana tree in which to raise the babes. The serpent taught them all they needed to know: how to grow yams, how to make fire and how to speak.[9]

Ophites

At first glance the concepts of the Far East, with its esoteric and transformative vision of the mythical dragon, are concepts that run contrary to the Christian vision – to which the dragon was something unholy and destructive. In their world view it was a death-dealer, a creature that was vicious and mean and ultimately infused with un-Christian practices. However, it would appear that this is a surface allusion. An undercurrent swam against the mainstream visions of both Orthodox and Catholic churches. There were those for whom the older ideas were not dead and gone, but worthy of incorporating with the new. As the Church grew in power and fervour, serpent lore was a vital act of defiance in the face of a tyrannical overlord (at least that's how gnostics viewed the god of the Bible).

In the mysteries of the gnostic sects we find a warping of Judaic/Christian/Grecian and Egyptian myth and philosophy. We find familiar elements here: the Orphic egg, the Cosmic Serpent, the Ouroboros, the Mother Goddess, the triple principle and the reoccurring law of threes. These concepts gave rise to the mystical orders and ideas of the Ophites, Gnostics, Hermetics and such-like. These intellectual ingredients were mostly fused in the syncretic cauldron that was the city of Alexandria.[1]

Hermes Trismegistus is the merging of Egyptian Thoth and Hermes: a syncretism that probably occurred around the 2nd century BCE. Trismegistus means thrice great, a term applied to Thoth even earlier than this. By the time that the *Corpus Hermeticum* was compiled, Hermes Trismegistus was an entity in its own right. He was a sage and scholar, god and philosopher. In Alexandria, and the religious syncretism that took place there by the 1st century CE, there were many who followed the teaching of this god. The *Corpus Hermeticum* was a manual for achieving *gnosis*: the righteous inspiration of the divine. The texts survived in fragments until they were transcribed by the magician, Marsilio Ficino, scribe to Cosimo Medico in the 1400s. It's one of the major influences of the hermetic resurgence of the medieval era.[2]

The city of Alexandria was a meeting place of cultures, trade, philosophy and power. In its hey-day it attracted scholars from across the ancient world and had a burgeoning library. Science and mathematics were practiced and elevated by people such as Hypatia, the female scholar.[3] It was also a centre for Christian philosophers who set out the terms of the future church and consolidated Christian texts (as well as the likes of Arius, of the Arian heresy).

The Gnostic sect of the Ophites venerated the virtues of the serpent-dragon. In their beliefs genuinely un-Christian concepts rise from the bolt hole: creation was a series of emanations, and from a union of masculine and feminine was born a 'Christ'. This was a supposedly incorruptible light, of which some fell back into the material world to become an androgynous being known as Sophia (knowledge) or Prunikos. From this a series of further emanations arose as it came into contact with the cosmic waters of creation. One of the beings birthed from this union was named Ialdabaoth, the Demi-urge. Along with its six kin, these seven deities ruled the seven heavens. Ialdabaoth in turn was forced to procreate and birthed the serpent named Ophiomorphus (*Nous*). From this came soul, spirit, but also envy, wickedness and ultimately death.[4]

Ialdabaoth then sealed the world within his presence and said there were no other gods but he, no other deity above him. When he saw the first man, Adam, he grew jealous and created Eve to trick him. But Sophia appeared as the serpent and tempted Eve with the apple. Via this medium, Adam and Eve fell into the material realm. For this insult the serpent was cursed by Ialdabaoth.

The Ophites derive their name from Ophis, or serpent. Some refer to them as pre-Christian, although their creed blends elements of Pagan and Christian concepts. There were numerous Ophite sects, amongst them the *Sethians, Peratics, Justinians* and *Naassenes*. The latter took their name from the Hebrew word for serpent, *nachash,* which is *Naas* in Greek. This snake was connected with *Nous,* the mind (*Ophiomorphus*).[5]

The diagram of the Ophites was a schematic of their cosmology. Seven circles represented the seven heavens, each ruled by an Archon (of whom Ialdabaoth was one). All these heavens were enclosed within the perimeter of another circle: the Ophite serpent in ouroboros form, which some also named Leviathan. Within the centre-most circle lay the wicked realm of Behemoth, which was a grouping of Pagan underworlds, such as Hades and Tartarus – and therefore classed as a kingdom of evil.[6]

One of the few recorded Ophite ceremonies is a peculiar rite in which a serpent was placed upon an initiate's naked body. It was guided to glide from breast to the genitals, eliciting strong emotions in the initiate, and propelling them into gnostic ecstasies. Serpents were also allowed to slither over bread (and likely other goods) for it was felt that their doing so purified and consecrated the object. They were also respected for their healing properties.[7]

According to the Ophite, Justinus, there existed three primal powers: the good abiding in the kingdom of light (equated with Priapus). Next is Elohim, the god of heaven (the Demi-urge). Elohim falls for the third power (Eden) a naga-like female. The union between them produces twenty-four angelic beings, named after trees in the garden of Eden. Each of the cosmic partners favours twelve of each. A third of each of these groups is favoured over others. Baruch, the Tree of life, is Elohim's favoured, while Eden prefers Naas (known here as the Tree of the Knowledge of Good and Evil). The angels of Elohim are responsible for the creation of Adam and Eve, while those of Eden bring famine and misery. Naas seduces Eve and infects her with the sin of lust, then has sex with Adam, apparently corrupting him. The tale goes on, mixing pagan and Christian tropes to create a tale that the scholar, Hippolytus described as 'monstrous'.[8]

Agathodaimon

The Sabians of Harrān (in modern day Syria) worshipped a being known as Agathodaimon alongside Hermes and Pythagoras; not as gods, but as prophets. The sect's ideas were informed by ancient Babylonian cults as well as Hermeticism and Neo-Platonism and their cult survived into the 11th century. Agathodaimon was a beneficent daimon, known as the 'Good Spirit of Alexandria' and was sometimes depicted as a bearded serpent, wearing a double crown. He often bears the semblance of Serapis, the half-serpent god of Alexandria.[1]

The male daimon was often accompanied by the female, *Agathe Tyche* (identified with *Isis-Thermuthis*). These two are sometimes shown together with their tails knotted in the *Nodus Herculeus*, the Herkules Knot. They are also carved alongside the caduceus and were aspects of the same being: the feminine/masculine and Third Principle that permeates ancient culture. In this light their association with the caduceus makes sense.[2]

Agathodaimon has his roots in the protective *genus loci* serpent of the home. He was honoured throughout Greece and Rome, but mostly his worship flourished in Egypt, with Alexandria being the centre of his cult. During the syncretism of the centuries during the Hellenistic and Roman periods, many religious concepts came together to form newer traditions. Influenced by Grecian philosophy and ancient Mediterranean traditions, new cults formed.[3]

Partly a product of this process, Agathodaimon was already firmly rooted in a theological tradition that extended back to ancient Egyptian and Hellenistic religion. His symbolism was multi-layered and absorbed that of other deities: from Dionysus and Serapis to the Egyptian creator gods, Shai and Kematef. In Greece he was also known as Zeus Meilichios and associated with fortune. This is due to Hellene influence in Egypt, where Serapis was viewed as a form of Zeus. He was also linked with Asclepius and was believed by some Islamic scholars to have been his teacher. A Libyan shrine portrays Agathodaimon as a bearded serpent below a bust of Serapis. Beside the serpent is carved a pine *thrysus* (pine-cone topped staff). It shouldn't surprise us that, according to Byzantine references – themselves purporting to be quoting earlier texts – Agathodaimon was the father of Hermes Trismegistos.[4]

In magical texts of the time, Agathodaimon could be summoned by the use of seven sacred names. He also featured in the instruction for reciting the *Heptagram* – in which he was honoured as supreme deity.[5] His seven magical names were: Harponknouphi, Brintantênôphri, Brisskulma, Araouazarba, Mesenkriphi, Niptoumi and Khmoumaôphi. Some of these conceal the true names of certain deities, such as Horus and Osiris. He was also known in Greek as Psoi (from Pshai/Shai), and is sometimes named as: *Psoi Pnouthi Ninthêr,* Agathodaimon: god of the gods.[6]

The Greek 'magical papyri' summon him as Eternity and name him Aion (a name that featured in Hermetic and late Platonic theology). In a ritual to bless a magical ring the following is written as part of the invocation:

> *"What Aion nourishing, and what Aion rules the Aions? One deathless god. You are the begetter of all and assign souls to all and control all, King of Aions and lord."*[7]

Theologian, Iamblichus refers to him as Kmêph: the intellect that thinks itself. His nature is manifold and profound. The self-intuiting intellect, the mirror that beholds its own reflection. In this light he is the equivalent of the Platonic Demi-urge, an ordering principle born from chaos but ordering all it made manifest from the realm of pure mind. An Islamic text tells that Agathodaimon espoused the first five principles as: creator, reason, soul, space and void.[8] In this we can glimpse references to much more archaic cosmological serpents, such as Egyptian Sito.

Abraxas

Forming a hybrid symbolism, the gnostic deity known as Abrasax was carved onto gemstones, carried by members of some gnostic sects. His imagery made it as far north as the Roman town of Chesters, on Hadrian's Wall. Macrobius says that according to the oracle of the Clarian Apollo he is identified with Hades, Zeus and Helios.[1]

Also known as Abraxas, he was hatched by a cock from a serpent's egg. In form it appears as a basilisk, with a cockerel's head, a knight's torso, and serpent legs. This being is found in the texts of Simon Magus. Its name was a replacement for that of the creator, whose true name is unmentionable. Basilides says that Abraxas was chief of the three-hundred and sixty-five heavens (Basilides laid great store in 365 – a number that Abraxas totalled in numerology and his name was likely designed to achieve this total). The Persian Sun God was named Abraxas and it might be that the origins of his worship can be found here. Some amulets and gems reveal him as Lord of Hosts, Ruler of All.[2]

The shield he holds in his left hand represents Sophia (as in *Pistis Sophia* – the goddess of philosophy). In his right he clasps a whip symbolising his right to assert dominance. Sometimes his shield is inscribed with the Greek letters for the Demi-urge: IAO. The Greek for Yahweh. In many ways Abrasax parallels Mithraic worship: Mithras was also a sun god whose name in numerology totalled three-hundred and sixty-five.[3]

Again, in this character we find a fusion of ancient and Christian ideas.

Chapter 5

What the Dragon Knows

Medieval alchemy was a revitalisation of the earlier gnostic traditions, some of which centred around the so-called Hermes Trismegistus (Thrice Blessed), itself owing much to philosophical Grecian and ancient Egyptian thought: where mercurial energies were stressed in serpentine imagery, and reinforced by the imagery of the dragon.

The image of the double-serpent features in a lot of art of this period. Sometimes in simple S-form, or a flowing W, with each terminal crested by a serpent head. It appears in ancient Aztec art, as the Plumed Serpent, stunningly visualised in turquoise. Similar double-serpents appear in Pictish art of the 6th-7th centuries CE, and in Norse and Germanic art. In fact, double serpents sometimes fill complete intricacies of Celtic knot-work designs. They also appear in the hermetic tomes of the 1500s and 1600s, where they sit alongside another double serpent motif: that of the caduceus.

I'm not suggesting here that the double-serpent in Mexico possessed the same symbolism as that of the Pictish imagery – although the same psychological process may motivate their inception.

In ancient Greece an interesting tale is told about Tiresias, the blind seer who was deified by the gods. *En route* between Thebes and Glisas he chanced upon two battling serpents and attacked them with his staff. For this crime he was changed into a woman for seven years (another version of the story explains that Tiresias actually attacked the Serpent-Dragon, Ophis as he peered from a hole. The seer cut its head off and the place was known thereafter as *Opheôs Kephalê*, or 'snake's head'). On the eighth year he chanced upon them again and this time, when he struck them, he returned to the form of a man. However, his tribulations weren't over, for Hera and Zeus were arguing over who enjoyed sex most, man or woman. They decided to ask Tiresias because he'd been both. Siding with Zeus cost him his eyesight, for Hera blinded the poor man, but she blessed him with prophecy (if that can be counted as a blessing).[1]

Veiled within this myth are the dualistic concepts that run like a stream through serpent mythology. Thousands of miles away, in India, two serpent deities are named *Maha Devi* and *Maha Deva*. Their imagery, of two entwined snakes, is found at Nâga shrines.[2] Here the two serpents, are directly associated with another serpent cult.

In the earliest manifestation of the practice known as Tantra, the powerful spirits known as *nagini* were used to signify the principles of *yang* and *yin*. *Yang* is male, activity and lucidity, while feminine *Yin* is passive and obscure – the masculine is white, the feminine black. Each contains within it the seed of the other.[3] The notion of the dual principle, reflected in later philosophy, was refined in the vision of the dual serpent energy, that lay latent at the base of the human spine, in the practice of Kundalini (the name means 'coiled'). Tantric energy ties in with caduceus and serpent imagery at a sacred level. Sun and Moon, masculine and feminine, positive and negative, wind round a central axis, a phallus or stem, to create a Third Principle. Kundalini energy is the flow of inner energy, visualised as double serpents that wind up the spine (trunk or staff). It's clear that these ideas have similar roots. In alchemy the serpents of the caduceus represent two metaphoric streams bound by Mercurial powers.[4]

The imagery is familiar, and puts us in mind of the caduceus. The serpents winding around the upright spine, like the serpents of Hermes' staff. The caduceus has an earlier precedent in the dragon god, Ningishzida.

Ningishzida – Prince of Dragons

The ancient Sumerian deity, Ningishzida is both dragon-king and prince of dragons. References about him come from fragments incised on clay tablets. He is praised as a god who ascends the sacred mountain to enter the realm of the gods, but he can also descend into the Underworld – earning him the title, 'Chair-bearer of the Underworld'. Thus he mediates between the Otherworld and the world of the mortals. He is a judge and meditator, armed with great knowledge (presumably gathered because he intercedes and travels the realms – alongside Dumuzi he judged the dead in the Underworld). He is also a god of field and meadow, who is said to unite both snakes and dragons. The temple of Eninnu was built in his honour. He is further identified with the period of the new sun between the winter and summer solstice.[1]

A vase from Gudea bears a vital clue to the function and form of this deity. He is not only dragon-like but is symbolically represented by a pair of snakes (*Bašmu*) which entwine about a lone rod. One of his titles is *ù-mu-un mu-zi-da,* Lord of the True Tree – a term also applied to Tammuz. The true tree is, of course, the World Tree, which the rod signifies (the World Tree is also the way of rising or ascending into the realms of immortals, as Yggdrasil, the Norse version, attests). The two serpents hint at a deeper philosophical meaning. This is the caduceus, which forms another winding branch of serpent philosophy. In later Mesopotamian art these serpent guardians were replaced by artfully weaving branches.[2]

In some images, Ningishzida holds the caduceus rod in his right hand. He is even described as the right-hand sceptre god, and is depicted as a tall figure with serpents rising from his shoulders, or coiled about him. He is also sometimes symbolised by a horned serpent and was identified with the constellation of Hydra.[3]

Together with the god, Tammuz, his cultic centre lay at Gishbanda, which lay between the ancient city states of Ur and Lagash. Tammuz was also known as Dumuzi. His name means 'Son of Life'. His father is Ea and he is famous for being the lover of Inanna. When the goddess descended into the Underworld, she was punished by the gods for sitting upon Ereshkigal's throne. She was hung upon a hook and slain. However, two magical beings called Gala-tur-ra and Kur-gur-ra accepted Inanna's body in return for easing Ereshkigal's labour pains. Using special herbs they healed Inanna and brought her back to life. But, attempting to flee the Underworld, she was halted by the gods. They decided that, in order to leave, Inanna needed to give them a replacement. The goddesses saw Dumuzi, reclining upon his throne and acting as though nothing of consequence had happened. In rage she offered him up, and thus Dumuzi and Inanna divided the year between them, each taking their six month sojourn in the Underworld. However, Dumuzi didn't yield willingly to this bequest and attempted to flee in the form of a snake.[4]

This pairing of Ningishzida and Tammuz is intentional and reflects a unity of opposites. Together they guard the door of heaven but also have dealings in the Underworld. The use of double-serpents and rod in early iconography might even suggest that the snakes represent both gods guarding the sacred tree. The reference to him being the god of the right-hand sceptre might possibly be an inference to his being set upon the right-hand side of the early caduceus symbol (with Tammuz to the left).[5]

In one legend, Adapa is a great sage, searching for the gods who have disappeared from earth (and being gods of vegetation and the meadow, they are sorely missed). Ningishzida and Tammuz approach the high god Anu, to appeal on the sage's behalf.[6]

This duo also appear as wives or husbands to each other, pointing to an ambiguity of sex and to their role as symbol/*Logos*. They *are* the caduceus in its early form, representing the concept of masculine and feminine, each borrowing a little from the other and thus forming the Third Principle. In Sumerian cosmology, creation comprised of a series of emanations; waves of manifestation that began with the union of heavenly masculine and feminine principles. The first being was Anu, who was also the heaven, whose realm was guarded by Tammuz and Ningishzida. Each emanation contained the dual principles, which by their unity formed a Third Principle: a self-begetting deity (not unlike the Egyptian Sito).[7]

The Vase from Gudea

The Grecian Caduceus

In many ways Hermes mirrors Ningishzida. He is the divine messenger who can ascend and descend between the Heavens, Earth and Hades. It was Hermes whom people addressed on lead tablets to ask favours of the gods, before they cast them into the sacred waters. He was their direct line to Mount Olympus: a bridge between worlds, and between mortals and gods. Hermes was often the god who was impeached to pass on messages to dead relatives.

Hermes was known as Mercury amongst the Romans and as Turns to their neighbours, the Etruscans. His father was Zeus and his mother, Maia, was an old-time earth nymph and a messenger of Hera's. In the soap opera of the Olympians, Maia was reduced to the status of a shy nymph hiding in a cave, visited by Zeus while his wife was asleep.[1] After ten moons she conceived a child, he was wayward, tricky but gifted and possessed eloquent speech. Hermes has been traced to being a proto-Olympian serpent god.[2] Like many such beings, he was born of the Earth Goddess and was a god of the Spring. It was in the Olympian dramas that Hermes assumed the attributes he was worshipped for in Classical times. As well as bearing the caduceus, he was portrayed with winged sandals and helm, to symbolise his travelling between the realms.

His name derives from piles of stones that marked crossroads and boundaries. These piles became pillars, some of which were topped with bearded faces, representing Hermes. In this early form he appears as a strong image of phallic masculine fertility. The placing of these *hermes* denotes him as providing a sacred function at crossroads and boundaries. As time passed he was portrayed as a youth.[3]

Encompassing opposites, he was beneficent to travellers, but he also honoured thieves. He is a god of eloquence, speech, poetry, verse, and writing. He brings the messages of the gods and he can explain them, even in dreams (a favoured medium for such sacred relays). His eloquence can provide words of beauty, but they can also conceal treachery and cunning. While protecting cowherds he also gives honour to merchants. He was known as *Logos* to the Greeks and followers of the Orphic mysteries burned frankincense in his honour.[4]

By the time he is equipped with the caduceus, his symbology is well defined. In the Homeric Hymn to Hermes, dated from the 6th Century BCE, we are told that he holds the "rod of blameless peace". The balance denoted by the symbolism of masculine and feminine principles had been accepted as the rightful symbol for a mediator such as he. He was androgynous and the pair of serpents reflected the opposites apparent in nature. Therefore his staff is Hermes as *Logos*. He represented a fecund but rational power that permeated everything.[5]

If we mention Hermes, we must also mention Thoth. Across the Mediterranean, this Egyptian deity became synonymous with Hermes, as the Greek and Egyptian cultures greatly influenced each other. Thoth shares many characteristics with his Grecian counterpart. He's the god of writing, of speech, augury and intelligence, magic, and he's closely associated with the Moon. As an astronomer he knows the stars intimately. Importantly, in this context, he's a mediator and a psychopomp who guides the dead to *Duat*: the halls of the dead. He mediates, like Hermes, between mortals and gods. Thoth is also sometimes portrayed holding the rod of Asclepius, and in this aspect is a protector from illness.[6]

Thoth was a self-created deity, said to be the personification of the mind of Ptah. As we've seen, this is a role also fulfilled by Sito, the cosmic serpent. He was also known as the tongue of Rĕ. In ancient Memphis there lay a book, said to have been written by Thoth's own hand. It was stored within his temple, and guarded by an immortal serpent. Thoth directed the creation of the Khemenu, which were four opposing pairs of beings. Four were apes and four were serpent-headed frog-legged humans. Though each possessed the properties of masculine and feminine, the pairs represented profound concepts that gave rise to the world's creation: primal waters, infinite space, darkness and invisibility. These were reputed to be the oldest of the gods. They formed a sacred eight, or Ogdoad and were worshipped in the city of Khemenu, which was known to the Greeks as Hermopolis: Hermes city.[7]

The Sceptre of the Dragon-King

On a Mesopotamian seal, dated to between 2500-2000 BCE, the goddess Inanna stands upon a hybrid dragon. She holds aloft the sacred caduceus. Even in this tiny image the artist managed to convey a sense of the goddess's presence. She isn't just asserting her might over the dragon, it is the dragon that elevates her.[1] Here snakes and dragons are united. The Serpent lore is apparent.

We have traced the symbol back to an ancient and enigmatic pair of deities – one of whom is Prince of Dragons. A millennia later, the caduceus appears amongst imagery of the gods of the Grecian pantheon. It's from their culture we take its name – where it was also called the *kerykeion* and the Staff of Hermes. Many scholarly books state that Hermes is a later incarnation of the Sumerian Dragon Prince. Hermes carries the same symbol as Ningishzida and both appear to exhibit certain traits in common. They are both associated with the Underworld and pass between the realms (no easy task, not even for gods).

As we've seen, Hermes is the messenger of the gods, psychopomp, giver of laws and teacher of languages. The staff he bears is said to function as a symbol of mediation, it symbolises fertility and the balance of opposing forces. Though this definition is much older than the Grecian Hermes, in both deity and symbol we find an amalgamation of several concepts. This syncretism occurred again in Alexandria, where he appears as Hermes Trismegistus whose writings formed the basis of

Hermeticism: a doctrine of esoteric evolution and spiritual growth that was practised into the seventeenth century CE (and finds a resurgence in the modern era).[2]

The Greeks had a number of origin stories for the caduceus. One was that Hermes created the staff after chancing across two battling snakes. Another is that it originally belonged to Iris, Hera's messenger, but it was gifted by Apollo in exchange for Hermes' gift of a lyre. Either way its meaning is drawn of deeper substance. The staff has its own mythology built on older foundations: the ruins of civilisations long disappeared.[3]

Tanith, the Phoenician Goddess, serpent lady and consort of the sky god Baal, becomes part of the symbol in the 1st century BCE, as she stands between two serpents of the caduceus. Tanith can be identified with a double deity, *Sêd-Tanit*, a janus figure of masculine and feminine entities. Goddess of the heavens and the Moon, she was honoured at the ancient city of Carthage.[4]

The Caduceus can be said to represent a union of opposites, while the cone or sphere in some versions signifies the unity of consciousness. Others have suggested that the imagery appears to reflect the neural activity in hypnagogic states, and therefore represents the two hemispheres of the brain encasing the penal gland. Roman scholars could symbolically account for the constituent elements of the caduceus: the wings meant diligence, the serpent, wisdom, the staff was power, the cone or helmet presaged lofty thoughts. It could also imply the union of elements: Earth being signified by the staff, air by the wings with the serpents representing fire and water.[5]

The rod was used as a 'sender' or elaborate wand in ceremonies such as that attributed to Zeus Meilichios. Perhaps its power was seen as acting as a sort of divine aerial between the realms of immortals and mortals. It is similar to the *rhabdos*, which is a forked wand bound by a chthonic serpent. Similar twinned serpents, flowing to form an interlace also appear in

India, carved upon the *Nâgakal* stones. Their symbology is not dissimilar.[6]

There is an obvious overlap with the Rod of Asclepius here too. Indeed, the pharmacy logo used across Europe today is a cross between healer's staff and Caduceus. Originally the rod of Asclepius was a lone serpent that wound around a staff. It symbolised the potent healing properties of the god. Of course, the roots of this serpent symbology might be from natural observations (the shedding of skin and the snake's poison providing an antidote). The use of the double-serpent imagery and its association with healing can also be found in examples of Islamic art from Anatolia.[7]

The Caduceus has other intriguing parallels: the Hittites of ancient Syria worshipped a triad named a *semeion,* which consisted of the thunder god, Hadad (Adad), and Atargatis, a fertility goddess who was likened to Demeter. This pair were equated by the Syrian scholar Lucian, as Zeus and Hera united by the symbol that lay between them, known as their son, or daughter (which hints at both). This was the *semeion*. However, Roman inscriptions name this Third Principle – for its father is Jupiter (Zeus), its mother Venus (Hera) and therefore their offspring is Mercury ie; Hermes. The symbol that represents the Third Principle looks like a caduceus with the serpents reduced to snaky S's.[8]

In Hindu tradition, the caduceus is linked with tantric energy. Two serpents form parallel streams around a central trunk/phallus/stem. In the practice of Kundalini the human spine is the shaft, around which serpent energies climb. Both ideas stem from same root. Tantric energy ties in with caduceus and serpent imagery at a sacred level.[9]

Here we must step back and take a breath. Let's strip this down to its essentials: a triple symbol of storm god, earth goddess and a Third Principle – in this case an *androgynous deity of mediation*. We have seen this pattern in other sections of this book. The masculine and feminine dragons permeate myths and folklore and we see the same pattern in the ancient battle stories of the thundering dragon slayer.

The dragon inhabits liminal worlds, it can fly between heaven and the underworld, and therefore is seen as a mediator. It functions as a bipolar symbol that unifies to create a Third Principle. As we see in the case of Hermes, who is known as the *Logos*. This is something that goes beyond the concept of deity. Although *Logos* was used to mean reason and discourse,[10] in this sense it is the animating principle that unties everything – the soul of the world. This revelation is symbolically expressed as both deity and emblem.

It is no wonder that many tales hint at the wisdom of the dragon. It is most venerable, ancient and it penetrates the very core of being.

Chapter 6

What Came First, the Serpent or the Egg?

Dissecting the Dragon

In this book we've covered a lot of ground. It's pretty evident that the serpent-dragons of old were especially revered and formed the vital component of ancient philosophical and cosmological theories. We've examined dragons from many countries and time periods. We've seen that certain core ideas hinge much of the lore that surrounds the dragon.

The dragon comes from way down in the depths of the cosmic waters, rising to break the surface in various guises. Yet the imagery is surprisingly consistent throughout the centuries. The myth of the triumph of the sky god (Order) over the mother earth, or her wayward child (Elemental forces/Chaos), has endured throughout the millennia. Each version works toward the same outcome. To break the myth down into its constituent ingredients we have:

1 – A serpent dragon borne of the cosmic waters, living in a loch or other body of (cosmic) water.

2 – A sky god, armed with thunderbolt or dragon slaying hero who comes to smite the monster.

In these conflicts the masculine is ultimately dominant. In the older versions of this myth a creative process takes place at the instigation of the victor and from the remains of the conquered.

The battle is an event so great that it is imprinted in the human myth of many cultures. This raises many questions. Sometimes it feels like a patriarchal conspiracy, echoing the notions of Marija Gimbutas, the archaeologist and proponent of the theory that patriarchal gods displaced matriarchal goddesses, reigning in their creative powers. Is this what these myths suggest? A consolidation of tribal power? The dominance of the male, warrior-based Indo-European society over a more feminine, and gentler society that predated this?

We've also seen that there's another body of myth, which generated a more esoteric and dragon-friendly approach. The essence of this particular body of mythology is:

1– A masculine principle.
2– A feminine principle.
3– The two unite and a third is born. The third is often androgynous, a fusion of both principles working harmoniously. The Third Principle.

In essence this reflects the caduceus and yin-yang, a concept familiar to many of us today. From Battle to Caduceus, the concept is the same. However, the resolution is very different.

Is this an older strata of belief? Could two strands have co-existed? Some hold that the dragon, as a negative creature (like Tiamat or Vrtra), was a concept that came to Europe from Greece. There is no way of proving such a hypothesis. After researching this subject for many years it's my contention that a much older strata of mythology once existed in Europe. This earlier strata was more in-line with the dragon's eastern counterpart.

I have barely skimmed the surface of the amount of serpents and dragons, dragonesses associated with wells and springs across Eurasia – from China to the Highlands of Scotland. This idea of wells, springs and bodies of water being associated with serpent-dragons saturates the older strata. Although corrupted in part, it remains telling that such places were centres for healing. They were also places where oracular dreams were sought and knowledge was to be gained. That succeeding cultures adopted this symbolism/concept to their own ends, is highly likely, especially where people already knew of similar beliefs from their own homelands. To place a date when this occurred is pointless, as successive waves of settlers added to or brought similar myths. However, it is certain that, in the West, Christianity and the Catholic church sought to both eradicate and appropriate such ideas where it suited them.

However, to isolate the constituent elements of the symbolism that comes with the well we get:

1 – There is a well/cosmic waters/waters of life and death. It is a nurturing and healing place.
2 – A sacred tree is centred at the well.
3 – The fruit of the tree are magical, often yielding knowledge or eternal youth.
4 – A serpent dragon guards or is the essence of the well.

Although the dragon slaying prototype was embraced by the Christians, we've seen that its imagery is much older. It can be traced in the earliest civilisations, from Mesopotamia, ancient Assyria, pre-classical Greece and many other regions. In India, Vrtra is the cause of a drought, it holds waters back. However, in Chinese mythology the dragon overcomes inundations and comes to the aid of the people.[1]

Given the timescales and distances involved here, how did this mythology remain so cohesive? The Finnish school of scholastic thought held that myths which occur with similar manifestations, amongst different peoples, must have a common root. They must have originated at one place and spread from there, diffusing from this locus. This progress was not constant – for example, books would affect the spread because they could be transported over a greater distance, and begin their own small-scale diffusions as they influenced those who came into contact with their content. Proponents of the Finnish method concluded that the dragon myth radiated from Sumeria, with the Babylonian dragon myth of Tiamat as the diffusion point.

However, the 6,000 year old Chinese dragon statue was made thousands of years before the Babylonian dragon myth. The Yangshao culture find shattered this theory. Particular attention seemed to have been given to the details of this dragon by its maker: it was covered with arrow-shaped shells. From this region the Shang Dynasty eventually developed (1600-1100 BCE), a people who claimed to have been born of the dragon. Other images of similar antiquity have been found, including one in Mongolia, which was about 5,485 years old.[2]

It's possible that some of these ideas were diffused over areas of the Eurasian landmass at an early point in history. It's well documented that Indic and Iranian myths shared a common root, and ideas must have been exchanged during the times when the great city states – those of Mesopotamia and the Harappan culture of the Indus valley thrived in the 2nd millennium BCE. And there is a strong case for the diffusion of the Dragon Slaying myth by Indo-Europeans, spreading east and west with the so-called Indo-Iranians – who colonised what later became known as Persia between 2000-1000 BCE.[3]

However, the problem with the whole Indo-European diffusion theory arises when we begin to search other countries untouched by Indo-European peoples.

It is assumed that the first peoples to reach America did so via the Bering strait, crossing a now submerged landmass between the two continents. Other theories have also been put forward and the dating is still a contentious issue. A tentative estimate gives anything between 13,000 to 300,000 years ago, with human tribes spreading and settling throughout the length of the continent.

However people arrived in the continent, serpent lore appears to have gone with them. In many accounts, myths of the North American Great Serpent associate it with thunder. Sometimes it even represents quick-darting lightning.[4] However, the inference of serpent and thunder is interesting. We have seen in the previous chapters that The Oldest Battle is wrought between a sky god, specifically a thunder god against the Earth-bound dragon. The hero versus the monster. The representation of order over chaos, patriarch over matriarch seems to dominate images in the West, while in the East the inference is that the forces that the dragon represent are beneficial and respected.

In Cherokee myth we find a story of the giant, horned serpent Uktena (keen-eyed) sent by the Little Men to kill the Sun after it sent sickness to destroy the humans. The Pawnee referred to the sound of the storm as the hissing of the Great Snake, while the Algonquins thought that lightning was a serpent spat by Manitou. The North American Ojibwe tell of a manitou chief that dwells beneath the waters of a lake. Mishebeshu is the lord of the watery world, and appears as a horned serpent-dragon. His name is best not mentioned, but if needs be then wait till the winter cold has frozen the waters of his realm first. Not that the dragon is evil, rather it is indifferent to human needs and desires.[5]

A tale is told of a band of hunting Sioux warriors who slew a great serpent. They were ravenous and all but one of them ate the snake. Upon waking, the chief discovered that they'd been turned into half-serpent beings. The youth who had declined the feast was unchanged and became their intermediary, as they explained to their kinsfolk what had happened. Every summer the snake-people would return to the village, shining in their new coats. It is said that, even many decades after the event, people of their village would never a harm a serpent they chanced across, preferring to offer conversation instead.[6]

Further South, in the lands of the Toltec and Aztec of modern Mexico, reverence was given to Cihuacoatl, the serpent woman whose thunderous call was an omen of war. She was an Earth Goddess, summoned by women during childbirth. With her partner, Quetzalcoatl, she created new people at the beginning of the Fifth Sun. She is identified with the goddess Coatlicue (serpent skirt) a fierce serpent goddess who ruled over life and death. Coatlicue birthed the Sun God, Huitzilopochtli, while her daughter, Coyolxauhoui, was the Moon. She's depicted as a savage goddess, wearing serpent skins and sporting a necklace whose beads are human hearts. Like Kali Yuga, she gives life and snaps it away. Her children, the Sun and Moon, were joined by four-hundred others, who were rebellious and were therefore banished into the heavens to become the stars.[7]

There are many myths about the plumed serpent, Quetzalcoatl. One is that he and his shadow side, Tezcatlipoca (smoking Mirror), chanced upon the goddess, Tlalteutli as she was walking alone across the primal waters. They decided they wished to create something from her and each grabbed two of her limbs and ripped her apart. From her remains they fashioned the earth and sky, and also the gods. They then paid homage to the goddess and they formed the grass, trees and flowers from her hair, while from her eyes they fashioned springs and fountains, from her mouth the rivers and great caves, her nose the valleys, and her shoulders became the mountains. The goddess wept ceaselessly, not because of what the Quetzalcoatl and Tezcatlipoca had done to her, but because she craved human hearts, and she would not be quiet until she was sated by human blood.[8]

Quetzalcoatl was a deity held in reverence by many tribes. As well as forming a pair of serpent gods with Cihuacoatl, he is a deity in the Hermes aspect. For it is Quetzalcoatl to whom the birth of science is attributed. His spheres of influence include medicine and agriculture. He invented the calendar, writing and books. He was attributed to the morning star, Venus. He is a huge feathered serpent, with plumes of many colours. Like the Great Serpents in other parts of the globe, he is a dragon. Quetzalcoatl is all-powerful and pervasive, influencing many aspects of people's lives. His similarity to Thoth and Hermes is obvious.[9]

The Amazonian Shipibo recount a legend of the Great Anaconda, known as Ronin, the Great Mother. In artworks the cosmic serpent is heavily referenced as an embodiment of all pattern throughout all time. The paint itself is seen as a divine conduit for these motifs. Sometimes a circular motif is used to represent the great serpent. To the Desana tribe of the Amazon, the Milky way is seen as a manifestation of the cosmic anaconda, the life-bearing serpent of creation.[10]

From the group of many islands that lie within the Torres strait, above the Northern Australian continent, come several curious serpent stories. Amongst them are the male and female siblings who were the first ancestors of a clan which took a snake totem as their emblem. On the island of Dauan, lived a harmless snake known as the Kogia, after the legendary serpent of the same name. Originally a man, he turned himself into a serpent. There is a tale that a youngster brought a snake to keep as a pet, and hid it in a cave. It grew to gigantic proportions and soon incurred the wrath of the boy's tribe, as it stole all their food each night. Fleeing its cave the giant serpent roved from island to island.[11]

Norinori is an ancient ancestor serpent from Paira, now known as Cape York. He also roamed the sea and the islands, swallowing any canoes and their occupants as he went. Upon reaching Badu he found a spot he felt was perfect for him to settle. He lived in the ground, in a labyrinthine home of many openings. One day Norinori chanced upon a party of women who were looking for leaves to weave. He was mesmerised by one of the women named Staurab, and chased her. Norinori kept appearing from his many holes to block her passage and finally, once she was exhausted, he gulped her into his mouth and brought her into his lair. Although she was his captive, the serpent went forth every day to find food for her. While it was away she scraped at the dirt of her prison, seeking to dig her way free. Her husband came to search for her and heard her singing.

He called out, and she replied, bidding him to stamp his feet. Where she had scraped the earth free, the ground was thin and after stamping for a time it gave way, revealing Staurab who pulled her to safety. Returning to find his prize gone, Norinori daubed his face with a line of crimson from the middle of his forehead to the tip of his nose, and another from his right nostril diagonally across his face to the apex of his jaw. Then he put a headdress of feathers on and flew into the sky in pursuit. However, two Argan eagles told the couple not to worry, and they swooped upon the serpent, lifting him high into the air, then letting him fall into the ocean. It is said Norinori broke into three pieces, each part becoming an island.[12]

Africa is a place of origins and heartland of the human species. Ethiopians were long known to the Greeks, as were other North African tribes. Numidian warriors made up a large contingent of Hannibal's army in the second Carthaginian wars of the 2nd century BCE. Once upon a time, Ethiopia was governed by a tyrannical serpent. It was immense in size, with sharp teeth as long as the tallest of men and its name was Arwe. The slayer of this monster didn't resort to violence with weaponry, but instead he used his head. First he brought the beast a white lamb and fed it. After it had eaten and grew thirsty, he gave it the white juice from the euphorbia tree, which was poisonous.[13]

The Fon of Benin call the cosmic serpent Aido-Hwedo, and it carried the Creator Goddess in its mouth. It was seen as a rainbow serpent that girded the universe. The cosmic serpent of the Woyo people of the Congo brought rain, and was the daughter of the Great Mother. It was known as Bunzi and was also symbolised by the rainbow. The Lunda tribe called it Chinawezi, and it was married to Nkuba, the lightning. When he rumbled in the sky above, she allowed the waters below to swell and rise. Many African tribes liken the rainbow to a cosmic serpent. In the Fon pantheon there also appear a pair of creator deities who accessed the great serpent power – Da Zoji and Nyohwè Ananu. Together they begat the pantheon of earth gods. To the Tutsi and Hutu tribes of Rwanda, the Goddess Imana created everything. She also offered to reveal to man the secret of immortality, but he fell asleep. However, a canny serpent had overheard their conversion and pretended to be the man. Thus Imana told the serpent the secret of shedding its skin and being reborn. The Fipa tell a similar tale, in which their creator came to earth and asked who wanted to learn how to be immortal. Only the serpent was awake, and so it alone learned the secret. In Nigeria, Effion Obassi, the Creator, fashioned the Moon from a stone plucked from the head of a huge python. The Venda people count a python named Tharu as their ancestor. The Baga of New Guinea also see pythons as the manifestations of their ancestors.[14]

Here we are lightly skipping across the earth, but these examples serve to show that these phenomena aren't restricted to those descended from Indo-European ancestors. And yet, could such concepts have taken their precedents in a deeper strata of human evolution? Modern academics shy away from the idea of the transference and continuation of beliefs. However, there's much evidence to counter such assumptions (and these have been adequately covered in this book, whose content serves as a testament to the continuation of belief over many millennia).

Certainly Marija Gimbutas believed that one of the earliest carved images, the spiral, directly referenced the serpent. Pointing to motifs of coiling double-spirals as suggesting some form of early cosmological or creation myth. The imagery is very suggestive of later concepts such as *yin yang*. Ancient Grecian creation myths include accounts of the primordial serpent winding around the cosmic egg. Images which some scholars, including Gimbutas, suggest appear in the archaeological record during the Eastern European Chalcolithic and Neolithic era. In these images the serpent spirals (or sideways S forms) curl around circles or eggs. The patterns suggest a current of opposing energies and a fluidity indicative of concepts such as the cosmic waters. Imagery of this nature permeates cultural crossroads societies such as the Cucuteni (dating between 4200-4050 BCE).[15]

It's obvious from a study of Grecian myth – for which we have a substantial amount of written reference dating into antiquity – that the Olympian pantheon were replacements for older deities, who themselves supplanted more animistic spirits. The reason that certain myths hold similarities is, perhaps, partly due to their diffusion with the people: from the earliest foragers, to the settlers and migrants who followed. When ancient tribespeople migrated, they likely encountered the beliefs existing amongst indigenous peoples of that region that were familiar to them. For example, in the Romanisation of Celtic deities, those that were similar to the Romans retained their original name, pre-fixed with their Roman counterpart. This also occurred in Greece, for example, there are numerous different Hercules, and different accounts of other gods, such as Apollo. Zeus *Meilichios* takes the place of a pre-Olympian *genus loci*. It's evident this is an ongoing process. Although morphed from their origins, their main players remained: the Mother Goddess' monster serpent and the sky god, known under various guises.

Amongst many of these peoples, animist practices were part and parcel of their spiritual life. The people who presided over such beliefs (and were perhaps directly in touch with the mysterious 'other') were wizards, witch-doctors – now usually referred to as shaman. The name is used as a 'hold-all' reference for practitioners of animism whose methods and results possess universal parallels.

It may be that the awareness of this core myth stretches back into the megalithic mind. The spirals and wave forms hammered into the sides of tombs, and are found in numerous sites throughout Europe could be our species' intuitive resonance and awareness of animistic forms. Most early beliefs took the form we might term *shamanistic*; denoting a tribal mode of belief that involved principles of animism, spirit worlds and the use of trance/hallucinogenics taken by an intermediary (shaman) on behalf of the community. Some have traced this type of religious practice back to the earliest known settlements of human habitation and ritual sites such as the caves of Lascaux (17000 BCE).

But can we discover any hints of the serpent-dragon motif in such ancient practices?

Amongst the many experiences of a shaman are those of death and resurrection. It is this ordeal that is a common feature amongst many practitioners. It is more than an initiation. For many it is a calling. Among the Australian Warramunga tribe the initiate or candidate underwent a spiritual process of endurance: they were sliced open and their internal organs were removed. A snake was placed inside their head, or body, and this endowed their healing powers. The Yakut have a tale that the first shaman was made of snakes. In another Australian tale, the medicine man reveals that, to initiate another, the master strips away their flesh and insides until the initiate is just a skeleton. He shrinks the skeleton to infant size and places him inside a bag. He then mounts the Rainbow Serpent and clambers up its body, where he ritually kills the initiate, tossing him into the sky. Next, he fills the candidate's lifeless body with small rainbow serpents, fresh water snakes and quartz crystals. The process is now ended and the Rainbow Serpent returns them to the earth. Snakes featured prominently in the costume of Altai shaman, and consisted of ribbons, some with eyes, some with three bodies and one head.[16]

Shamanism features as one of the earliest forms of spiritual belief systems on the planet. Although never unified, the various practices share many uncannily common features, despite being separated by great distances in both time and distance. We must also note that in regards to the latter symbolism centred around wells, similar elements are found in shamanic ritual. Shamanic practice still persists to this day in various parts of the globe. From South America to Siberia, Africa to Asia, shamanic beliefs share common elements, these include: otherworld encounters, trance/frenzied states, visions of serpents and world trees.

The move toward monotheism was a gradual process and there were precedent steps toward it. The anthropomorphising, and organising hierarchies of deities was a move along this path. It arose from the need to organise the chaotic nature of earlier, more intuitive non-systems of faith/belief/knowledge – this might reflect the inward-turned psychological mindset developed in ancient city-states, over lingering hunter-gatherer beliefs. With the arrival of anthropomorphic deities perhaps we are witnessing the solidification/codification of the human condition in god form. An internalising of the human condition is hinted at in the *sakta* practices of Hindu religion – which enables a deep awareness of the psychological aspects of the deities. *Yantra* symbols are meditated upon and each respective deity addressed is recognised as an aspect of the Self. Perhaps then, with the development of extended human settlements, we are seeing new forms of anthropocentric belief rising and the philosophical extensions of these ideas being extended over the centuries. The earlier animistic beliefs are reflected in the hegemonies of titans, giants, Vrtra, Tiamat etc. The recognition of the great forces of nature that belonged to the hunter-gathers.

Part of this older belief involved the serpent guardian of natural bodies of water, especially springs. However, this force was kept in check by the human gods, especially in the form of the sky god. From this we can see how the precedent is set for the Oldest Battle. In one respect it's the symbolic form that has been chosen to represent a dualism of nature and society. But I believe here we have the roots of a religious change and the rise of anthropomorphic deities dominating animistic spirits. And although we shouldn't see this change as a wholly violent struggle, its process was gradual and the animistic serpent beliefs received less precedence over time.

This apparent 'subjugation' of older forms of belief is documented in many ancient texts such as Indra's triumph over Vrtra – the dragon that holds back the water. As we've seen, this theme echoes throughout much ancient mythology. Whether this is purely the result of Indo-European tribal movements, or perhaps a shift in human consciousness remains to be seen. I'm inclined to suspect a little of each, one complementing the other. This neither rules out possibilities of archetypes, or the spread of mythic concepts via a medium such as the morphogenic field (see below).

At least, that's one reasonable hypothesis. One possibility. Not a truth, but an idea. But could it be that there is something much weirder going on here? Something that is very difficult for us to comprehend. When we hear of visions of twisting ladders that transform into serpents – a common hallucination amongst psychedelic voyagers and shamans – is this just a product of the imagination? Or an echo of the DNA helix of life itself?[17] Whereas psychoanalytically, Freud would have argued the Finnish School's case, Carl Jung would have pointed to the archetypal realm of the collective subconscious. Both image and myth, he would have said, could arise independently in different places.[18] Could it be that although these serpent-dragons were localised, they are also a core myth locked within the unconscious of the human species? Thus the stories moved with the people because they are manifestations of deeply human psychological processes. Archetypes.

The problem with the Finnish method is that it doesn't account for ideas such as archetypes of the subconscious mind, the collective consciousness or an intuitive underpinning of life itself. It doesn't account for origins in dreams or the independent invention of folk narratives. Mythical tales could even be the result of ritual, or the observation of heavenly phenomena such as comets, or the aurora or other electromagnetic phenomena in the sky. It could also be that we are all wired a certain way and therefore our ideas are guided along certain templates that are part physiological, part encoded in our DNA. Therefore for a similar event, even if it takes place in different regions of the world, a common conclusion might arise: the place our minds go to when we try to explain things. Rupert Sheldrake proposes that memory is inherent in nature, events and laws in the natural world are habit-forming. These 'habits' are dependent on what he calls morphogenic fields. Inter-species knowledge is 'transferred' via these fields. In this view, there is no central point of diffusion, but a species-wide awareness.[19]

Examining the dragon lore in this book we can see that a pattern emerges. A patten that is, I think, much deeper than the cultural dispersion of myth travelling with movements of tribal peoples such as the Indo-Europeans. This is not to doubt that ideas did travel. But the evidence suggests either a radical overhaul of the theory of the diffusion of mythic concepts globally, or points in the direction of a shared process of symbolism, an unconscious template that would seem to bolster Jungian theories of archetypes.

In one aspect the battle myth represents themes of the victory of order over chaos. Sky gods and divine heroes battle serpent-dragons that rear from the depths of the earth. Like Vrtra, they represent uncontrollable elemental forces. Powers such as earthquakes, floods and other natural events that would have terrified tribal peoples. The story of the god defeating the monster is therefore ancient and poignant. It can be translated as a triumph of good over evil, a concept that fed into Zoroastrian ideas of duality and the classification of good and evil – which subsequently fed Abrahamic myths.

The fact is that many serpent-dragons have Earth Goddess associations, or come from the depths of the earth, and are thus birthed by her. This feminine association, which we have seen evidenced in these pages, makes it hard not to reduce this to a battle of the sexes.

Beyond the Battle, we see this pairing of feminine and masculine imagery, which echoes through symbolism such as the caduceus, and forms the vital components of the Third Principle. However, the Battle mythology suggests a dominant role on the part of the masculine. The Celtic God, Taranis, bears upon the serpent, trampling it beneath the hooves of his horse – mythology is jam-packed with imagery of the female earth goddess rearing hideous offspring that are brought into line by male sky warriors. The imagery alludes to a particular sequence of mythological events.

If this myth does pertain to a patriarchal takeover, whether that be a result of Bronze Age machoism, or innate Indo-European ancestry, then it's interesting to note that the Battle is still in effect. If anything, the rise of the political conservative right, with its hankering for old style Christian values (Yahweh = a Sky God) – while at the same time more open-minded, dare I say liberal values, such as Feminism and progressive forward-thinking science are threatened by the rise of corporate populist politics. Right wing conservatism seeks to assert itself, thundering on about its sky god and, slave to consumerism, ridicules those who believe in environmentalism and the condition of the earth.

After all, many of these tales and lore we have examined here serve as evidence of the suppression of one form of religion by another. And in the Oldest Battle we have the evidence of that schism. While, enfolded in the strata of legend, the benign serpent remains – the serpent deities that are often counselled by priestess or goddess, usually at the source of waters. And here, I can't refrain from serving up another classic example, this time from Egyptian mythology: in the sacred city of Heliopolis, where the Great Serpent was worshipped under a number of names, the God Rě attacks 'the Slippery One', as they argue over who inherits the site. Rě agitates his 'brethren' in order to take Heliopolis for himself. He attacks the serpent with a harpoon but is overcome when it transforms into a curly haired maiden who then seduces the god. As well as this apparent serpent/female link, Rě's choice of weapon is revealing: a harpoon is used against ocean dwelling creatures. The dragon-slayer myth is repeated.[20]

Of course, it may well be that this battle was solely on the cosmic scale, as the myth relates. But what if these myths are reflecting something very pertinent about the human condition? That the Neolithic peoples, emerging from the hunter-gatherer era: settling and assimilating to the life of pastoral hierarchies were somehow aware that Paradise was done for. With the arrival of bronze, enter war-like deities reflecting war-like man. Check out the Alpine preponderance and fascination with warrior and weapon in Bronze-Age megalithic carvings... or Scandinavian petroglyphs of warships, decks crowded with fighting figures... *the hero has awoken*! Settled people have much more to lose. No longer moving from place-to-place humans take up arms to defend their plots of golden grain. Is this what these myths are telling us?

What if Western political mores of the present times have fudged the judgement of speculative historians? In the battle between the sexes, might we be talking about some revolution that never took place because it was never really there? The serpent gods and goddesses were just that. There was no golden age of equality and 'special knowledge'. There was no matriarchal society of peace-loving creatives. Woman was treated as badly then as she always has been, goddess or not. In this case, what if the myths are merely reflecting the reality of the time? The only women who were respected, for a time, were those in the religious fields, priestesses who served the function as oracles and seers at the well source. And what if men in a hard-living and war-like society reflected themselves in their stormy war-like deities – and the serpent, being something feared in many places, became a symbol for ill?

And yet, an excavated sanctuary in Parta, Romania, was found to be comprised of three chambers. Within it were found the sculptures of a bull-headed man and a headless voluptuous female.[21] These finds were dated between 5500 BCE and 4500 BCE (long before Indo-European migration). In Bulgaria, the early settlement of Slatina revealed a divine couple of the Neolithic period. They comprise of a bull god and female. Various assemblages were discovered here, including a central column beside a pit. This column may well have represented the *axis mundi*.[22]. Could this be some of the earliest evidence of the tripartite system which we see reflected in various cultures world-wide? If so, what does this mean? Was there a yearning for balance? A mediating influence that is reflected in the symbol of the caduceus?

Myth is something we invent and renew, something innate within us, a force in which core concepts are reclothed, personages renamed and ideas altered to fit the changing cultures that adopt them. Myth is important because it is intrinsic to the human condition. Through mythology symbolism is tried and tested. Symbolic language is part of being human, it is a deep, wordless language, the forms of which are never obvious, but layered in the subconscious mind and thus assimilated there.

But perhaps I am in error. Perhaps all these reflections of reality are invalid – the result of some innate propensity to explain the inexplainable. Dragons exist. Whether they be animist spirits, energies and manifestations of such, they possess a reality that is beyond 'real'. If we take the myths at face value, isn't that evidence enough?

Whatever the reason one thing is clear: we live in a fast-paced and rapidly changing world. We are surrounded by increasingly sophisticated technology. Yet how far have we, as human beings, truly come? In ancient Egypt, myths revolved around Apophis, the serpent that represented the chaos and void of the night, the serpent that swallowed the sun. Of course, the world was viewed very differently back then – and yet, viewed metaphorically, the myth retains its relevance and poignancy. It is still relevant.

The forces of destruction and creation in other parts of the solar system have been captured by telescopes hurtling through the void: colliding galaxies, supernovas, stars that collapse in on themselves to create inescapable black holes with holographic surfaces. Yes, Apep-Tiamat-Vrtra-Typhon-Python-Leviathan-Sito, whatever handle you wish to bestow upon the dragon – it still exists as a primal force… *an entity*. We all know the earth is a sphere, revolving around the sun, gravity chains us to the planet, our climate is precious, and pretty unique. But out there, beyond the glow of our atmosphere does the icy serpent encircle us still?

In this day and age we hear about the constant devaluation of meaning. Perhaps the ancient concepts detailed in this book can set a precedent and offer us insights into the great mystery, perhaps they can spark our interest, our innate intrigue in life itself, a life unclouded by consumerism and the follies of mainstream religion.

The dragon as a symbol is the perfect creature to epitomise the New Great Battle: the fight for the environment. The dragon was often benevolent and seen to represent the waters, the rivers, the very moisture in the air and clouds, the vital principle of life itself. It was also a symbol of evil and to the early Christians a manifestation of the pagan wilderness. It inhabited the burial mound where dark things lived.

Saint Guthlac dwelled within a burial mound in the fens of England, in the 700s. He was besieged by demons and his account is almost like a witch-doctor's journey to another world, a shamanic voyage. But in his case Nature is against him, and he symbolises the civilisation of the time – Christians believed they were bringing light to dark lands.

Everything is flipped on its head. It is arguable that today civilisation and humans are now the monsters. The ecological disasters of consumerist capitalism are the result of rampant industrialisation and pollution. Despite this, we are facing the resurgence of modern day Christian ethics that place man at the centre of the universe – the man god bowing to his sky god. But in these times we need the dragon. Like the shaman who is dismembered before they are reborn, so too the dragon. It was from the dragon's corpse that Marduk fashioned the world. But the dragon needs to be resurrected in all its glory. We need to adopt it as a vital symbol and an element of the times we live in – the struggle necessary to save our one world. The dragon is the perfect symbol for the environment in which we live and the symbol of our need for ecological reparation and change.

I hope you have enjoyed this Book.

Endnotes

Chapter 1: The Serpent From the Depths

Forged Within a Dragon's Thoughts

1. H. Frankfort – *Cylinder Seals*, 1939.
2. Bostock, John & Riley, H.T. – *The Natural History: Pliny the Elder, Book 91* Ch 16 (online via Perseus http://www.perseus.tufts.edu/hopper/text?doc=Perseus:text:1999.02.0137:book=24:chapter=91&highlight=dracontium.
3. Goldsmith, Elizabeth E. – *Life Symbols: as Related to Sex Symbolism*, Pg 102, 155 & Eliade, Mircea – Patterns in Comparative Religion, Pg 452, Lunar connections: 154-88. In gnostic concepts, shaped by both Christian and older traditions, there's mention of a pearl guarded by a *chaos dragon*. The quest for this precious stone was likened to that of the Christian Saviour, and in this context the serpent appeared in predictably negative fashion. However, the reference to the pearl is interesting, given its association with dragons in the East – Sheppard, H. J. – *The Ouroboros & the Unity of Matter in Alchemy*, Pg 83-96.
4. Goldsmith, Pg 155.
5. Sargent, Denny – *Naga-Magick: The Wisdom of the Serpent Lords*, Pg 16.
6. Campbell, John Francis – *Popular Tales of Western Scotland: Vol II*, Pg 369-70 – The tradition was known in Cornwall as *Gelin Nedir*.
7. Bostock, John & Riley, H.T. – *The Natural History: Pliny the Elder, Bk 29*, Ch 12. (online, http://www.perseus.tufts.edu/hopper/text?doc=Perseus:text:1999.02.0137:book=29:chapter=12&highlight=anguinum).
8. Allen, Judy, Griffiths, Jeanne – *The Book of the Dragon*, Pg 36.
9. Folkard Jnr, Richard – *Plant Lore Legends & Lyrics*, Pg 527.

10. Edwards, Cyril – *Nibelungenlied.* The German saga has older precedents, including the aforementioned *Volsungr Saga.*
11. Ananikiam, Mardios H. – *Armenian Mythology,* Pg 82.
12. Eliade, Mircea – *Patterns in Comparative Religion,* Pg 207-8.
13. Edwards, Ruth B. – *Kadmos the Phoenician,* Pg 40.
14. Zhao, Qiguang – *The Study of Dragons in the East & West,* Pg 128-9.
15. Vinycomb, John – *Fictitious & Symbolic Creatures in Art,* Pg 79-80.
16. Zhao, Pg 85 & Sara Kuehn – *The Dragon in Medieval East Christian & Islamic Art,* who provides much evidence of the use of dragon imagery for protective use, but samples can be found on Pg, 22, 26, 35.

Symbol of War and Warlords

1. Zhao, Qiguang – *The Study of Dragons in the East & West,* Pg 84-91. Eliade, Mircea – *Patterns in Comparative Religion,* Pg 207-8.
2. Such sacrifices have been found across the ancient world, and the notion stems from practices grounded in the Neolithic. The sacrifice became guardian and protector spirit of the building.
3. Vinycomb, John – *Fictitious & Symbolic Creatures in Art,* Pg 84-6, 90.
4. Sara Kuehn – *The Dragon in Medieval East Christian & Islamic Art, Dating*: Pg 36, Banners: Pg 40-1.
5. Kuehn, Pg 36.
6. Vinycomb, Pg 81-2.

In the Wastes the Wild Dragons Roam

1. Qiguang Zhao – *The Study of Dragons in the East & West,* Pg 126-7.
2. Charles Russell Coulter and Patricia Turner – *Encyclopaedia of Ancient Deities,* Pg 85.

3. L. Sh. Mikayelyan, Pg 232.
4. Mardios H. Ananikiam – *Armenian Mythology* (Myths of the world Vol VII – Pg 62, 77).
5. Should we be surprised to discover that she is the Queen of *Azi-Dahaka* and therefore assumes the role of Queen of Dragons?
6. Mardios H. Ananikiam – *Armenian Mythology* (Myths of the world Vol VII – Pg 8, 22).
7. Mike Dixon-Kennedy – *Encyclopaedia of Slavic & Russian Myth & Legend*, Pg 92-3.
8. See, *The Oldest War*.
9. Byock, Jesse L. – *The Saga of the Volsungs.*
10. Bloom, Harold – *Beowulf.*
11. *Czech Folktales* – Josef Baudiš.
12. See Airchaeology.org and Surrey Archaeology Bulletin 483.
13. See Slayer's Slab – https://www.atlasobscura.com/places/slayers-slab
14. Qiguang Zhao – *The Study of Dragons in the East & West*, Pg 41.
15. Paul Newman – *The Hill of the Dragon*, Pg 185 (also Knucker).
16. Margaret Clunies Ross – *A History of Old Norse Poetry & Poetics*, Pg 109.
17. This version taken from, *Encyclopaedia of Celtic Mythology & Folklore* – Patricia Monaghan.
18. Monaghan, Patricia – *Encyclopedia of Celtic Mythology & Folklore.*
19. Alan Temperley – *Tales of Galloway; The White Snake.*
20. It should be noted that the tale mentions that the snake rested its head in a pool known as the Boat Wheel. Legend has it that this was a pool where a crock of gold was protected by the Devil.
21. James Reuel Smith – *Springs & Wells in Greek & Roman Literature*, Pg 211.

22. This version of the tale from: *The Pursuit of Dairmuid and Grainne – Society for the Preservation of the Irish Language* (M.H. Gill & Son, 1887).
23. Patricia Monaghan – *Encyclopaedia of Celtic Mythology & Folklore.*
24. Edward Gwynn – *The Metrical Dindshenchas,* in the Poem 'Berba' – Pg 62 (Gaelic) and 63 (Eng. Trans).
25. From the snappily titled: *The Great Folly, Superstition, & Idolatry, of Pilgrimages in Ireland; especially of that to St. Patrick's purgatory. Together with an account of the loss that the publick sustaineth thereby; truly and impartially represented* – John Richardson (J. Hyde, 1727).
26. This version from *St Patrick's Purgatory: A Medieval Pilgrimage in Ireland* – St. John D. Seymour, Pg 8-9.
27. – Such was the strength of this belief that in the 1600s a pilgrim to the island, Ludovicus Pyrrhus used considerable funds to dig amongst the ruins on Saints Island to locate this door. He actually believed he'd found it, but this sacred passage to Purgatory proved to be the old cellar. Ludovicus returned to his native Brittany – described in John Richardson's account.
28. John D. Seymour – *St Patrick's Purgatory: A Medieval Pilgrimage in Ireland,* Pg 57.
29. *Encyclopaedia of Celtic Mythology & Folklore* – Patricia Monaghan.
30. Christiaan Corlett – *The Prehistoric Ritual Landscape of Croagh Patrick,* Co. Mayo.

All That's Contained Within A Word

1. John Vinycomb – *Fictitious & Symbolic Creatures in Art,* Pg 57-108.
2. See, *The Serpent That Encircles The World.*
3. Qiguang Zhao – *The Study of Dragons in the East & West.*

4. Something similar appears in Slavic myth – which ultimately derive from the east via Scythian ancestry: Scythian tribes bridge a gap between East and West and were influenced by art from either end of their diaspora. They took these art-forms and cultural references and made them something unique to their own culture. The later nomadic tribes of Huns and the Mongols in turn influenced Viking and Germanic art. This might explain why Norse dragons often have whisker-like appendages on their mouths (See Qiguang Zhao – *The Study of Dragons in the East & West* – Pg 19-20).
5. Judith Jesch – Ships & Men In the Late Viking Age, Pg 127.
6. The Town of Worms derives its name from the *Lindwurm*: the dragon that conquered the city, made famous by the tale of his slayer, Siegfried.
7. J. F. Campbell – *The Celtic Dragon Myth,* Pg xxiv (Introduction).
8. Patricia Monaghan – *Encyclopaedia of Celtic Mythology & Folklore,* Pg 377.
9. Kévin Tembouret – *French Folklore.*

Serpents of Hearth & Home

1. R.T Rundle Clark – *Myth & Symbol In Ancient Egypt,* Pg 50-56.
2. R.T Rundle Clark – *Myth & Symbol In Ancient Egypt,* Pg 239-45.
3. The logos-word and god of magic, R.T Rundle Clark – *Myth & Symbol In Ancient Egypt,* Pg 244-5.
4. Generally mentioned in *The Cult of the Serpent,* by Balaji Mundkur. Also *Indian Serpent Lore: Nagas in Hindu Legend & Art* – Jospeh Vogel and *Armenian Demonology: A Critical Overview* – Garnik Asatrian. There's evidence of the veneration of serpents in pre-Christian Baltic households, a belief that extends into the modern era.
5. Harrison, Jane Ellen – *Prolegomena.*

6. Margaret de G. Verrall – *Mythology & Monuments of Ancient Athens*, Pg xxvi- xxxii.
7. See, *The Oldest War*.
8. M. L. West – *The Orphic Poems*, Pg 121.
9. Margaret de G. Verrall – *Mythology & Monuments of Ancient Athens*, Pg xxvi- xxxii.
10. M. L. West – *The Orphic Poems*.
11. *Pausanias: A description of Greece* – translated by, Jones M.A & Ormerod, H.A (William Heinemann, 1918) Pg 123-5.
12. Margaret de G. Verrall – *Mythology & Monuments of Ancient Athens*, Pg 103.
13. Diodorus Siculus – *Histories Book II*, 42: 4.43.4 (Pg 27 of Oldfather's Translation).
14. Balaji Mundkur –*The Cult of the Serpent* contains many more examples of serpent handling and cults.
15. R.T Rundle Clark – *Myth & Symbol In Ancient Egypt*, Pg 239-45.
16. This is the conclusion drawn in *Indian Serpent Lore: Nâgas in Hindu Legend & Art* – Joseph Vogel's exhaustive study of this phenomenon.
17. Early Illyrian traditions linked serpent, Moon and female/ goddess throughout the region. *Zmijar* were Illyrian wizards versed in the secrets of snakes.
18. Detailed in *The Greek Origin of the Caduceum: Æsculapius* – Arturo G. Rillo, Pg 389-93.
19. This imagery is similar to that of Sirona from the lands of the Gauls.
20. Harrison, Jane Ellen – *Prolegomena* Pg 18-9.
21. E.A Wallis Budge – *Osiris & the Egyptian Resurrection, Vol 1.*
22. John Wilkes – *The Illyrians*, Pg 245.
23. Epicurus Fragment (from Epiphanius), found at www. Perseus.com
24. Sara Kuehn – The Dragon in Medieval East Christian & Islamic Art, Pg 78.

25. Mikayelyan, L. Sh.
26. *The Ouroboros & the Unity of Matter in Alchemy* – H. J. Sheppard.
27. Jane Ellen Harrison – *Themis; a study of the social origins of Greek Religion*, Pg 269-70.
28. Sara Kuehn – *The Dragon in Medieval East Christian & Islamic Art*, Pg 57-9.

Getting Cosmic

1. Vinycomb, John – *Fictitious & Symbolic Creatures in Art*, Pg 84.
2. Simpson, Jacqueline – *European Mythology*, Pg 130, 133.
3. Sara Kuehn – *The Dragon in Medieval East Christian & Islamic Art*, Pg 88-9.
4. Dixon-Kennedy, Mike – *Encyclopaedia of Slavic & Russian Myth & Legend*, Pg 16-7
5. Milošević, Nikola – *Slavic Gods*.
6. Dixon, Pg 258.
7. Milošević. According to the author of this document eating carp was said to induce Epileptic fits.
8. Dixon, Pg 280.
9. Zhao, Qiguang – *The Study of Dragons in the East & West*, Pg 8.
10. Frazer, James – *The Golden Bough*, Pg 84-5.
11. Goldsmith, Elizabeth E. – *Life Symbols*. Pg 151, 154. Zhao, Qiguang – *The Study of Dragons in the East & West* – The book examines the difference between East and Western dragon-lore.
12. Zhao, Pg 130-1.
13. Zhao, Pg 32-3.
14. Piggott, Juliett – *Japanese Mythology*, Pg 93-5.
15. Zhao, Pg 6-7, 23, 28, 46.
16. Goldsmith, Pg 41-4.
17. Zhao, Pg 15.

18. Collins, Anthony – Karahan *Tepe* – Entire Article: Collin's well researched paper also has imagery of the archaeology of the site.
19. Coulter, Pg 421.
20. Vogel, Pg 49, 192-8.
21. *Ogdoad* refers to a group of eight creative forces that were believed to be a vital part in the process of the world's creation. These Eight primal deities were, Nun and Nunet (primal waters), Heh and Hehet (Infinite space), Kek and Keket (darkness), Amun and Amunet (invisibility). They formed a great mound at Khemenu so that Reh or Ra the Sun God could rest as he traversed the heavens. It was also supposed that these eight merged to form the supreme god, Amun. At Hermopolis Thoth/Hermes is also linked to their worship – *Gods of Ancient Europe* – Barbara Watterson, Pg 179-80 & Feliciano, João Pedro – *The Agathos Daimon in Greco-Egyptian Religion*.
22. Feliciano, João Pedro – *The Agathos Daimon in Greco-Egyptian Religio*n, Article.

Dragon Slaying Saints

1. Qiguang Zhao – *The Study of Dragons in the East & West*, Pg 122-3.
2. The site of Uffington Castle was used from around 800 BCE and was re-used during the Romano-British period.
3. See, YouTube: Dragon Hill Mystery Conclusion – School of Archaeology, Geography and Environmental Science.
4. https://www.airchaeology.org/2019/02/17/dragon-hill/
5. Another intriguing dragon site is that of uncovered a small cave in the hill, upon which sits the ruins of St. Catherine's chapel. At the time of writing excavations have yet to analyse soot deposits within the cave (workings from the existing line also affected it and steam-train smoke may well confuse the data). Carvings within the small cave are said

to be Christian and speculated to date to the 14th century CE, possibly indicating a shrine, or hermit's cell. However, most investigations conclude that this isn't the oldest strata of its use. Given the ancient name of the place, Drakeshill, and the location of a healing well at its base (Artington Spring), which was reputed to cure sore eyes, we might suspect some form of ancient dragon ritual here too. see: https://guildford-dragon.com/mystery-of-st-catherines-hill-continues-as-sparse-new-evidence-emerges-from-cave-discovery-talk/

6. George Penny – *Traditions of Perth,* Pg 321.
7. Margo Todd – *The Perth Kirk Session Book 1577-1590,* Pg 151.
8. J. Ross – *The Book of Scottish Poems, Ancient & Modern,* Pg 51.
9. Lewis Spence – *The Legends & Romances of Brittany,* Pg 278-82.
10. Lewis Spence – *The Legends & Romances of Brittany,* Pg 365-6.
11. Claude Lecouteux – *Demons & Spirits of the Land: Ancestral Lore & Practices,* Pg 21.
12. There are those who suggest that Arthmael was in fact King Arthur. This idea is based on the translation of his name to derive, Bear Prince. However, it can also mean wolf-prince, or might even reference an armband. Themes of saints vanquishing dragons is a common trope in the West, and we'll investigate this phenomenon in a later chapter. See: *Lives of the British Saints* – S. Baring Gould & John Fisher.
13. Áge Avenstrup & Elisabeth Treitel – *Icelandic Fairy & Folktales.*
14. The myth of Adam and Eve: the corruption of the female, is actually paralleled in a Togo myth from Africa. In this the high god, Mombote had created forbidden fruits and a serpent led the first couple to eat it.
15. The Virgin Mary is sometimes illustrated treading upon a serpent in Catholic sacred art, an act emulated by many

saints and priests. Here she has defeated the serpent, ie: evil.

16. I imagine that it was worshipped under another name, and may well have been an image of Ba'al, Yahweh's main competitor in the region at the time.
17. Sara Kuehn documents many examples of this in "The Dragon in Medieval East Christian & Islamic Art."
18. See, *The Alchemy of Dragons*.
19. Anne Ross – *Druids: Preachers of Immortality*, Pg 17-8.
20. Simon the Magus was born in Samaria in 53 CE. His father was a sorcerer and as a youth Simon followed in the footsteps of an Arabian mystic called Dositheus. He eventually gathered his own band of followers and many legends were told of his miraculous powers. His ideas formed the core of many gnostic sects. Predictably, Biblical accounts downgrade his abilities (scholars think that the Simon Magus of the Bible isn't that same as the Gnostic father). See, *Gnosticism, its History & Influence* – Benjamin Walker, Pg 136-9.
21. Kees Veelenturf – *Visions of the End & Irish High Crosses*.
22. See, *The Serpent That Encircles the World*.
23. Qiguang Zhao, – *The Study of Dragons in the East & West*, Pg 55.
24. See – *The Oldest War*.
25. John Vinycomb – *Fictitious & Symbolic Creatures in Art*. Pg 73-4.
26. This might put one in mind of the leonine god of Time, Aion, also known earlier in Mithraic religion as Zervane – this is because there appears to be a direct continuity and absorption of these ideas into the corpus of Mithraism and later Gnostic philosophy. See, *Origins of the Caduceus* – A.L Frothingham.
27. J.A MacCulloch, George F. Moore – *Myths of the world (of all races), Vol-7*, also Mikayelyan, L. Sh. – *Various Aspects of*

the Image of a Dragon-serpent in Armenian & South Caucasian Sculpture.

28. www.duchas.ie

Chapter 2: The Oldest War

1. Apsu and Tiamat procreate and the first male and female forms of life are born into the cosmos: Lahmu and Lahamu, who are described as dragons and being the first emanations. *Sumerian Liturgical Texts* – Stephen Langdon, also, *Encyclopaedia of Ancient Deities* – Charles Russell Coulter and Patricia Turner.
2. Takayoshi Oshima – *The Babylonian God Marduk*, Pg 348-60.
3. *An Illustrated dictionary of Gods, Demons and Symbols of Ancient Mesopotamia* – Jeremy Black & Anthony Green.
4. See Takayoshi above.
5. See Coulter & Black above.
6. Takayoshi.
7. This information comes from two sources: Nomination Dossier for Inscription of the Property on the World Heritage List January 2018 (Ministry of Tourism, Republic of Iraq, 2018): Pg 25,27 and https://www.livius.org/articles/place/babylon/etemenanki/
8. This phenomenon is well documented (Penglase, Greek Myths & Mesopotamia, Pg 3. Takayoshi, Pg 351 and Fontenrose – *Python*, Pg 149). She was also known as Mother Hubur, which was the name used to refer to an underground river – S. H. Hooke – *Babylonian Art*, Pg 101.
9. Black & Green.
10. Behemoth is then Apsu in the Biblical revision of this story.
11. Hugo Radau – *The Creation Story of Genesis*, Pg 35, 3-7, 68.
12. Black & Green.
13. Barton, George – *Tiamat*, Pg 16-22.
14. The description of Oannes could well reference Neo-Assyrian figures of bearded figures clad in fish-skins. These

are said to represent the *apkallū*, or seven sages. These figures featured in religious art from the Kassite period (1730 BCE) into the Seleucid Empire (312-63 BCE), proving the longevity of the motif. The figures often flanked doorways, and images were found buried beneath floors, hinting at their protective and magical properties. The figurines were prescribed in ritual and supposed to be buried in groups of seven: a magical and sacred number since early times in Mesopotamia. There were seven gods, seven demons, the temple of Bel at Babylon possessed seven levels, and of course, seven sages. The seven sages belong to ancient Babylonian traditions and they were said to exist in pre-flood times. Texts tend to disagree on their names, and the cities to whom they gave their names. Sometimes they wear fish skins, other times they appear as demoniacal winged-griffins (see, *An Illustrated dictionary of Gods, Demons and Symbols of Ancient Mesopotamia* – Jeremy Black and Anthony Green).

15. Barton, Pg 3.
16. The Chaldeans were said, by Herodotus, to be the Priests of Bel.
17. Again Barton, Pg 3.
18. John Day – *Yahweh and the Gods and Goddesses of Caanan*, Pg 78-9.
19. Black & Green.
20. Day dedicates a whole chapter to this in Yahweh & the Gods & Goddesses of Caanan, Pg 68-90.
21. Lester L. Grabbe – *Ancient Israel*, Pg 156.
22. There is a body of linguistic evidence to suggest that Yahweh's enemies, Tannin and Leviathan, are different aspects of the same entity. A similar pattern applies for the enemies that Ba'al counters: Yamm, Tunnanu, Lotan. Again these all conform to *Tiamat – The Ugaritic Baal Cycle – Vol II* – Mark S. Smith & Wayne T. Pitard.

23. The Biblical account of Yahweh, in the Old Testament, describes how he defeats the dragon Leviathan. Though similar to the myth of Marduk and Tiamat, the myth actually echoes ancient Canaanite mythology, and parallels the stories of Yahweh's main contender in the region for the role of High God: Ba'al. This god's conflict with Lotan is most likely the original source of this mythos (there was much competition between the followers of both camps). Yahweh also defeated Rahab and Tannin, which are other names for Leviathan. It's been pointed out that the historicisation of the divine conflict with the dragon and the sea occurs in several parts of the Bible. The Egyptian Pharaoh is likened unto a dragon, and the dragon Rahab is sometimes used as a reference to Egypt – Day, John – *Yahweh and the Gods and Goddesses of Caanan*, Pg 19, 99, 103.
24. Scholars suggest that the texts are the result of a long oral tradition ranging from the 1800 BCE to the beginning of the Mid 2nd Century BCE. See, *The Ugaritic Baal Cycle – Vol 1* – Mark S. Smith, Pg 1.
25. There is a fusion of both the following references where it felt that, considering the myth it made more sense. *Ancient Israel* – Lester L. Grabbe and *Religious Texts From Ugarit* – N. Wyatt, Pg 115.
26. *Encyclopaedia of Ancient Deities* – Charles Russell Coulter and Patricia Turner, Pg 502. Also Debroy, Bibek (Translated by) – *Mahabharata, Vol I.*
27. Fontenrose – *Python*, Pg 195-208.
28. Julius Eggeling – *Satapatha-Brâhmana*, Pg 164-6.
29. West, M.L – *Indo-European Poetry & Myth*, Pg 260.
30. Eggeling, Pg 164-6, Fontenrose, Joseph – *Python: A study of the Delphic Myth and its origins*, Pg 386, Coutler & Turner Pg 500.
31. Said in some texts said to be Vrtra's parents.
32. Fontenrose – *Python*, Pg 451.

33. Note the similarity with cultures in which a giant is the primal world source, and from whose body the earth and all life upon it is fashioned.
34. Fontenrose – Python, Pg 196.
35. *Origins of Vedic civilisation* – Kenneth Chandler, Pg 6.
36. Chandler, Pg 6.
37. Jane McIntosh, – *The Ancient Indus Valleys*, Pg 23.
38. *Measuring the Harappan World* – Jonathan Mark Kenoyer (Full article) and McIntosh – *The Ancient Indus Valleys*, Pg 12, 40, 82.
39. Johnathan Kenoyer Article, *Measuring the Harappan world*, and Vedic mention, McIntosh – *The Ancient Indus Valleys*, Pg 34.
40. Kenneth Chandler, *Origins of Vedic Culture*, Pg 2,6, 14-25 and *Measuring the Harappan World* – Jonathan Mark Kenoyer.
41. *Encircler*: Kuehn, Pg 87, 146, *Apep*: L.F.C – *Gods and Goddesses of Ancient Egypt*, Pg 67-71.
42. Fontenrose – *Python*, Pg 121-25.
43. In later myths Ahi Dahaka becomes Zahhāk (Zohak). In medieval Persian folklore the myth of hideous sea serpents called Ajdahā (Azhidahakā) were feared by sailors and fishermen alike. These terrible monsters had seven heads and thrived in the stormy oceans.
    Sara Kuehn – *The Dragon in Medieval East Christian & Islamic Art*, Pg 54.
44. Kuehn, Pg 87-88.
45. Coulter & Turner, Pg 28.
46. Hinnells, John R – *Persian Mythology*, Pg 54.
47. There are a confusing array of names for this hero as he was adopted by successive and neighbouring cultures. They include, Thita/Trita and Atar, Fredon and Garshasp/ Keresapa and Vahagn – Their tales do differ, but what unites them is they all fight *Azi Dahaka*. To confuse things further the beast sometimes goes by different names, for

example, in the myths involving Trita this beast is called Visvarûpa – who, in Indian myth, is the son of Tvashtri, the smith god and therefore equatable with *Vrtra* – Hinnells, Pg 38-40.

48. Moore, George F. & Gray, Lewis H. – *Mythology of all Races, Volume VI*, Pg 320-22.
49. Moore & Gray, Pg 320-4.
50. Dixon-Kennedy – *Encyclopedia of Slavic & Russian Mythology*, Pg 289.
51. Kuehn, Pg 89-90.
52. Dixon-Kennedy – *Encyclopedia of Slavic & Russian Mythology*, Pg 289.
53. Matasovič, Ranko – *A Reader in Comparative I.E Religion*, Pg 66 quoted from, *The Birth of Vahagn – The History of Armenia* by Mowsēs Kcorenac'i.
54. West, M.L – *Indo-European Poetry and Myth*, Pg 246.
55. Moore & Gray, Pg 266.
56. Coulter & Turner, Pg 266.
57. More & Gray, Pg 327-8.
58. Grimal, Pierre – *A Concise Dictionary of Classical Mythology*, Pg 446-7.
59. Near the Orontes River.
60. There are two Corycian Caves, one is above Delphi, the other in Cilicia, a province of SE Turkey. While we are told that Delphyne's cave is in Cicilia, not Delphi, the reference to the Dragoness gives pause to wonder if this is a mistake.
61. Grimal, Pg 446-7, 122.
62. Bridgman, Timothy – *Hyperboreans*, Pg 25-9.
63. Bridgman, Pg 29.
64. Dempsey, T – *The Delphic Oracle*, Pg 157-9.
65. Penglase, Charles – *Greek Myths & Mesopotamia*, Pg 81-82.
66. Fontenrose, Pg 14.
67. Dempsey, Pg 63.

68. Penglase, Charles – *Greek Myths & Mesopotamia,* Pg 87, 88.
69. Fontenrose, Pg 16.
70. Dempsey, Pg 55-6.
71. Dempsey, Pg 49-50.
72. West – *Indo-European Poetry & Myth,* Pg 260-1.
73. Bloom – *Beowulf,* Pg 24-5.
74. Possibly Carlingford Lough. Binchy, D.A. – *The Saga of Fergus mac Léti.*
75. This is a strange name – Binchy thinks it is a misspelling, Calvert Watkins suspected a link between *-dris* and old Greek, **derk* – sight. A word that forms the root of Dragon.
76. Binchy, D.A. – *The Saga of Fergus mac Léti, Ériu Vol 16,* 1952, Pg 33-48. We have already seen that there were other dragon-slayers in Ireland, such as Fionn mac Cumhail – See, *In The Wastes The Wild Dragons Roam.*

Chapter 3: The Benevolence of Dragons

The Dragon That Guards the Sacred Tree

1. Dixon – *Slavic Myth,* Pg 268-71.
2. From, *Czech Folktales* – Josef Baudiš, Pg 71-97.
3. Lindow, John – *Norse Mythology,* Nidhoggr entry.
4. Yggdrasil is Odin's steed: Yggr being another of Odin's many appellations. This suggests that the tree itself is the medium by which the worlds connect and could be accessed by those with the knowledge to do so. It's well documented that certain aspects of the Odin myth are similar to what, nowadays, fall under the umbrella-term of 'shamanic practices'. The soul of a Tungus shaman will fly up the *tuuru,* their sacred larch, to retrieve souls nestled in the branches. Odin hangs on the world tree, for nine nights until the sacred runic alphabet is revealed to him – enforcing the idea that Yggdrasil, as Odin's steed, is the vehicle by which he travels to the many worlds. They're

either nestled in its branches or are found beneath its roots – See, Campbell, Joseph – *The Masks of God, Vol 1*, Pg 120-1.

5. Bauscatz, Paul – *The Well & The Tree*, Pg 12-20.
6. McHardy, Stuart – *The Quest for the Nine Maidens*, Ch 1.
7. Detailed in McHardy, Ch 2.
8. Spence, Lewis – *The Legends & Romances of Brittany*, Pg 59-60.
9. Entry for Dahut in Monaghan, Patricia – *Encyclopedia of Celtic Mythology & Folklore*, Pg 114-5.
10. Pomponius Mela, De Orbis Situ, Book 3:48 – https://babel.hathitrust.org/cgi/pt?id=mdp.39015042048507&view=1up&seq=127&q1=Gallizenæ
11. McHardy, Ch 5.
12. Same as above.
13. McHardy Ch 4
14. McHardy Ch 3.
15. Campbell, John Francis – *Popular Tales of Western Scotland, Vol III*, Pg191.
16. MacNeill Eoin – *Duanaire Finn*, Pg 170-88 "Adventure of the Men From Sorcha."
17. Campbell, John Francis – *Popular Tales of Western Scotland*, Vol I, Pg 24, Also McHardy, Ch 6.
    There is a Brehon tradition on the *Ile de Sein* that a coven of witches existed, known as the *groach'hed*. Again the parallels in language are evident.
18. McHardy, Ch 6. Also Fraser gives many examples of the corn-doll in *The Golden Bough*.
19. McHardy, Ch 3.
20. Dowden, Ken – *European Paganism*, Pg 181. Also Oehrl, Sigmund in "Re-Interpretations of Gotlandic Picture Stones Based on the Reflectance Transformation Imaging Method" from "Myth, Materiality & Lived Religion."
21. This is the grist of the point made in *The Masks of God, Vol III*, by Joseph Campbell, Chapter 1 & 3.

22. The Old Testament was compiled by Hebrew scholars during the 6th-8th centuries BCE. During the last millennium BCE the older Canaanite gods and goddesses were refuted and idolatry forbidden as the monotheistic religion was adopted by rulers.
23. March, Jennifer – *Cassell Dictionary of Classical Mythology,* Pg 394, Peck – *Harpers Dictionary of Classical Antiquities,* Pg 810.
24. Grant, Michael & Hazel, John – *Who's Who In Classical Mythology,* Pg 72, 87.
25. Grimal, Pierre – *A Concise Dictionary of Classical Mythology,* Pg 234, 190.
26. The *Graiae* appear like deities foreign to the Greeks themselves. Was Apollodorus correct to locate the garden in the far north? It's well established that the Hyperboreans were another name for the people who dwelled north of the Alps, ie; the Celts. Could these triple deities be reflections of folk observations of Celtic and Germanic deities? Could they reflect the Matronae (Mothers), whose triple-nature embodies the virtues of womanhood, from youth to old age? Triplicate orders and groups of deities also existed in Greece, so it cannot be proven but the link is worth considering. Section Refs: March, Pg 233, Peck, Pg 60, 740, 810.
27. March, Pg 394-6, Given the link with Nyx and Okeanus, it might be that the apples were a metaphor for a constellation of yellow stars that lay to the West, or the North.
28. Peck, Pg 810.
29. Litan – the wriggling serpent that is slain by the god, Ba'al – might form a linguistic parallel with Ladon (the suggested vocalisation of Lidān, while the Hebrew, *liwyātān* equates to Leviathan. This doesn't necessarily mean these are origins, but the similarity is intriguing. Wyatt, N – *Religious Texts From Ugarit,* Pg 115.
30. Fontenrose – *Python,* Pg 346.

31. Grimal, Pg 234, March, Pg 272.
32. March, Pg 447-8, 152.
33. MacLeod, Sharon – *Celtic Myth & Religion*, Pg 6, 11-2, 86.
34. See the Article "The Celtic Dragon Myth Revisited, by Joseph Nagy, in *Celtic Myth in the 21st Century: the Gods & Their Stories in a Global Perspective* – Emily Lyle.
35. Green, Miranda – *Bog Bodies Uncovered*, Pg 211.
36. Monaghan, Patricia – *Encyclopedia of Celtic Mythology & Folklore*, Pg 26-7.
37. Davidson, Hilda Ellis – *Lost Beliefs of Northern Europe*, Pg 68-70.
38. Eliade, Mircea – *Shamanism*, Pg 122.
39. Sara Kuehn – *The Dragon in Medieval East Christian & Islamic Art*, Pg 51-2.
40. Dixon, Pg 258. The *Simorg* was also a personal spirit dragon, protecting family and home.
    Zmaj – Old Slavic Gods, An anonymous Document that details much traditional Slavic and Serbian mythology. The Author is unnamed but the document is lengthy and informative.
41. Eliade – *Shamanism*, Pg 122, 271, Abyrga, Garide see Coulter, Pg 9. Phonetically, Sumur and Simorg do bear an uncanny resemblance.
42. Eliade – *Shamanism*, Pg 121-2. Also see, https://www.britishmuseum.org/blog/who-were-sogdians
43. Kuehn, Pg 66-7.
44. Zhao, Qiguang – The Study of Dragons in the East & West, Pg 17-26, 72-87.
45. Zhao, Pg 72-87 & Fraser – *The Golden Bough*, Pg 73.
46. Zhao, Pg 29-30.
47. Allen & Griffiths – *The Book of the Dragon*, Pg 41.
48. Eliade, Mircea – *Patterns in Comparative Religion*, Pg 165.
49. Grimal, Pg 421 & Fontenrose, Pg 366-373 & Smith, James Reuel – *Springs & Wells in Greek & Roman Literature*, Pg 177.

50. Kuehn, Pg 53.
51. Monaghan, Pg 67.
52. MacNeill Eoin – *Duanaire Finn,* Pg 191-3 & Article in Celtic Myth in the 21st Century: the Gods & Their Stories in a Global Perspective, by Sharon Paice MacLeod entitled "Gods, Poets & Entheogens.

    Another tale tells how the River Shannon's course was created by the *ollphéist*. Monaghan – *Encyclopedia of Celtic Mythology & Folklore.*
53. Ross, Margaret Clunies – *A History of Old Norse Poetry & Poetics*, Pg 168,244 & Newman, Paul – *The Hill of the Dragon: An Enquiry into the Nature of Dragon Legends,* Pg 185.
54. Smith, Pg 218, 426.
55. Zhao, Pg 101, it's also noted in the same text that water analogies are especially prevalent in Taoism, and the principle of water is likened to the flow of Tao itself.
56. Kuehn, Pg 53.
57. The origins of this word lie in the realms of sight, vision and clarity: see, *What's Contained Within a Word.*
58. Kuehn, Pg 53.
59. Tembouret, Kévin – *French Folklore,* Pg, 62.
60. Abbott, G.F. – *Macedonian Folklore,* Pg 260-5.

Mothers of Dragons

1. Mundkur, Balaji – *The Cult of the Serpent,* Pg 203-6, *ama-ushum-gal-anna*: Pg 187. Biehl, Peter F./Bertemes, François/ Meller, Harald (Editors) – *The Archaeology of Cult and Religion,* Pg 60. Vogel – *Indian Serpent Lore,* Pg 36, 76.
2. Mundkur, Pg 206.
3. As mentioned in the last chapter, the Fianna battle a dragon that arrived on Irish shores from Greece. Also bear in mind the significance of the word and its link with sight. *Dreco*: Gwynn, Edward – *The Metrical Dindshenchas,* Pg 15-7, 378-9.

4. Zmijar: Esmerović, Raif – *Cult of the Snake in Bosnia,* Pg 7. Tribe: Ananikiam, Mardios H. – *Armenian Mythology,* Pg 78, Anush: Pg 71, 78. In 190 CE their chief was *Argavan*. Another Armenian fable goes that the Devil created the dragon and made it purposefully huge, so that men would have to worship it. The fable states that in Sassanian times (224-651 CE), magicians performed a ceremony every three years to placate this devil, figuring that it wasn't evil by nature and could be converted to Christianity. There are also tales of human sacrifices made to black cave-dwelling dragons. (From *Armenian Mythology*).
5. *Ur-ur*: Cutillo, Brian & Rinpoche, Lama Kunga – *Drinking the Mountain Stream,* Pg 59. *Neolithic Serpent Goddess: Mundkur,* Pg 198. also, Gimbutas, Marija – *The Gods & Goddesses of Old Europe,* Pg, 101, 137, 146. Verbeia: Green, Miranda – *Symbol & Image In Celtic Religious Art,* Pg 25.
6. 'Myth, Materiality & Lived Religion', article by Sigmund Oehrl, Pg 141-90.
7. Psychoanalysts of the Freudian scheme see the lance of the dragon-slayer as a phallus, and a symbol of the masculine impaling the female principle. Jung said that the dragon is a symbol of our mothers but in a negative aspect. In this context the dragon does not function as good versus bad, but as unresolved conflict between the sexes.
8. Chauvinism: Zhao, *Qiguang – The Study of Dragons in the East & West,* Pg 61.
9. Milošević, Nikola – *Slavic Gods,* also Dixon-Kennedy, Mike – *Encyclopaedia of Slavic & Russian Myth & Legend.*
10. Sara Kuehn – *The Dragon in Medieval East Christian & Islamic Art,* Pg 90.
11. The inference made by Plutarch, in The Life of Alexander, Chapter 2, Sections 4-6 – in which Plutarch mentions that Philip did not dare approach the couch of his wife, Olympias. A serpent lay beside her. Another version he

gives is that Olympias was a follower of Dionysus, and through an ecstatic rite had a vision. A delegate was sent to Delphi to accept advice from the Pythia. In Chapter 3 Plutarch relates that Olympia lay with the God Ammon that appeared in the form of a serpent. The text also infers that Philip loses an eye when he steals a look through a chink in the door and beholds the god.

12. Dixon-Kennedy, Mike – *Encyclopaedia of Slavic & Russian Myth & Legend.*
13. Frothingham, A.L – 'Medusa, Apollo & the Great Mother' (Article), also Wilk, Stephen R. – *Medusa: Solving the mystery of the Gorgon,* Pg 24,45 *Gorgoneion,* Pg 95.
14. March, Jennifer R – *Cassell's Dictionary of Classical Mythology,* Pg 315.
15. Fontenrose – *Python,* Pg 100-4.
16. Fontenrose – *Python,* Pg 97-105.
17. Fontenrose – *Python,* Pg 115-9.
18. Winterborne, Anthony – *When the Norns Have Spoken,* Pg 56.
19. Winterborne, Ch 3 for overall idea and comparison. Fontenrose, Pg 13-4, and overview in Ch 6.
20. Williams, George M. – *Hindu Mythology.*
21. Eliade – Yoga. Pg 352. Parpola, Asko – *The Roots of Hinduism.*
22. Another important Indian myth tells the tale of the rivalry between two sisters, Kadru and Vinata. Kadru gives birth to a thousand snakes (*nagini*), while Vinata births the eagle (Garuda). Vishnu sends Garuda on a quest to snatch the divine nectar from the heavens. This sacred brew was known as *amrita* (translates as 'not death', ie: eternal) was guarded by two huge venomous serpents. Their tongues were like lightning and they resembled flickering flames with unblinking eyes. The bird Garuda blinded them with dust to steal some of the potent brew. However, the pot was snatched by Indra. The children of Kadru went to the place on the earth where the pot had been placed by Garuda before

its return to the heavens. There they licked the *darbha* grass that cut their tongues – this is why serpent's tongues are forked: Vogel, Joseph – *Indian Serpent Lore: Nâgas in Hindu Legend & Art.*

23. Coulter, Pg 421.
24. The brother of Krishna, Bala-Rama, took the form of a white serpent to go dwell with the Nâga in their underworld kingdom – Williams, George M. – *Hindu Mythology,* Pg 72.
25. Vogel, Pg 25-6.
26. Vogel, Pg 30-2, 134.
27. Zhao, Qiguang – *The Study of Dragons in the East & West,* Pg 8, 29. References to Nâga at pools are numerous but, Vogel, Pg 15, 23, 35, 58 & 91-2 provide a taster of the many examples. They also conform very much with the *Lung* dragon of the Chinese.
28. Zimmer, Heinrich – *Myths & Symbols in Indian Art & Civilisation,* Pg 72 & Sargent, Denny – *Naga-Magick: The Wisdom of the Serpent Lords,* Pg 19, 47.
29. Kuehn, Pg 53. Sargent, Pg 17. Vogel, Pg 36, 192, 220-46.
30. Sargent, Pg 20. Zimmer, Pg 66-8.
31. Aung, Dr. Htin – *Folk Elements in Burmese Buddhism,* Pg 111. Vogel, Pg 102-4.
32. Sargent, Pg 16. Aung, Pg 109-114.

    It isn't only the Buddha who is protected by the serpent. When Osiris reposed in the Underworld, he was enfolded within the protective coils of Nahaher, also known as Meher, the most ancient one. To rise whole once again, Osiris had to overcome the serpent by straightening it out (in some versions he has to cut it to bits). Only once he had defeated the serpent could he emerge from the cosmic mound. Clark, R.T Rundle – *Myth & Symbol in Ancient Egypt,* Pg 167-71.
33. Kuehn, Pg 36, 40.
34. Sargent, Pg 18, 21.

35. Parpola – *The roots of Hinduism*, Pg 286, McIntosh, Jane R. – *The Ancient Indus Valleys*, 44-5.
36. Kuehn, Pg 56-60.

The Immortal Healer

1. This story is distilled from, Campbell, John Francis – *Popular Tales of Western Scotland, Vol II*, Pg 361-4.
2. Campbell, Pg 365-6.
3. The Old Scots version related by Campbell again (same vol) Pg 362-3 – The Irish version is the most well-known and can be found in any volume on Irish Celtic Mythology.
4. Lucas, Mrs. Edgar (Translated by) – *Fairy Tales of the Brother Grimm*, Pg 197-201.
5. Seem *Serpents of Heart & Home.*
6. Rees, Alwyn & Brinley – *Celtic Heritage*, Pg 46.
7. Rees, Pg 244-5.
8. Foulke, William Dudley – *History of the Lombards: Paul the Deacon*, Ch XV.
9. Folkard Jnr, Richard – *Plant Lore Legends & Lyrics – Signatures*: Pg 150-60, *Arum Dracuticulus* & *Dracontium*, Pg 152.

Chapter 4: The Alchemy of Dragons

The Serpent That Encircles the World

1. Clark, R.T Rundle – *Myth & Symbol in Ancient Egypt*, Pg 239-44. In many regards Sito is so similar to Shai that I suspect they are one-and-the-same. See, Getting Cosmic.
2. Mundkur, Balaji – *The Cult of the Serpent*, Pg 74-6.
3. Roob, Alexander – *Alchemy & Mysticism*, Pg 330-33, Sheppard, H. J. – *The Ouroboros & the Unity of Matter in Alchemy*, Pg 83, 87.
4. Sheppard, Pg 87-9.
5. Mead, George Robert Stow – *Pistis Sophia*, Pg 322-3.
6. Sheppard, Pg 89.

7. Sheppard, Pg 89-90, Reemes, Dana Michael – *The Egyptian Ouroboros*, Pg 31-2.
8. Sheppard, Pg 84, 92-3, The Greek Philosophers of pre-Socratic thought used the phrase "Hen to Pan": the one, the all.
9. Pregadio, Fabrizio – *The Way of the Golden Elixir*, Pg 47-8, Goldsmith, Elizabeth E. – *Life Symbols*, 158.
   The dragon was more than a symbol for the Taoist's – who believed of the force of *Tao* itself was revealed in the appearance of a dragon. This hints at a deeper concept: that the energy of life-force *was* the dragon. Zen Taoists saw the dragon as cosmic spirit, emblematic of blissful enlightenment. In Mahayana Buddhism the dragon provided transport for Adi-Buddha; the supreme godhead manifested in the chant, AUM. It is from him whom all things manifest. In his Tantric personification he is known as Acala, and brandishes a sword, around which a dragon winds. A very early Chinese myth tells of Nü Kua, a creator deity who was an androgynous serpent with an ox's or sometimes human head. The figure is dualistic: *Nü* is the masculine and *Kau* the feminine, and the first human pair. Coulter, Charles Russell & Turner, Patricia – *Encyclopaedia of Ancient Deities*, Pg 15, Goldsmith, Pg 12-3.
10. Sheppard, Pg 94-5.
11. Sheppard, Pg 95.
12. Pneuma: Sheppard, Pg 83.

Orphism

1. Uždavinys, *Algis – The Golden Chain*, Pg 283-4.
2. Uždavinys, *Algis – Orpheus and the roots of Platonism*, Pg 39. Cornford, F.M – *Principium Sapientiae: The Origins of Greek Philosophical Thought*, Pg 89. There is a similarity between this myth and that of *Bendigeifriedfran* – the Giant, Bran the Blessed, of Celtic myth. In this Welsh legend, Bran's head is

housed by survivors of a vicious war with Ireland within a hall on the island of Gwales. There the company continue to be entertained by the wondrous head – This tale can be found in the *Mabingion* in the story entitled: Branwen, Daughter of Llŷr (*Branwen ferch Llŷr*).

3. Uždavinys, Algis – *Orpheus and the roots of Platonism, Daimon*: Pg 8, *anamnesis*: Pg 48, *Bakchoi & Lusios*: Pg 58, *Pharmaka*: Pg 38.
4. Uždavinys, *Algis – Orpheus and the roots of Platonism*, Pg 8, 41.
5. Uždavinys, *Algis – Orpheus and the roots of Platonism* & West, M. L. – *The Orphic Poems*.
6. Lies, Betty Bonham – *Earth's Daughters: Stories of Women in Classical Mythology*, Pg 4-5.
7. Epicurus Fragment (from Epiphanius) – www.Perseus.com, & Clark, R.T Rundle – *Myth & Symbol in Ancient Egypt*, Pg 54-6.
8. Sproul, Barbara C. – *Primal Myths From Around The World*, Pg 67.
9. White, Gordon – *Sky Ships*, Pg 94.

Ophites

1. Uždavinys, *Algis – Orpheus and the roots of Platonism*, Pg 47, 58 & West, M. L. – The Orphic Poems, Pg 26.
2. Lachman, Gary – *The Quest for Hermes Trismegistus*.
3. She was versed in the arts of science, astronomy, philosophy and her light was snuffed out by a mob of Christian zealots in 415 AD.
4. Walker, Benjamin – *Gnosticism, its History & Influence*, Pg 42, 49-51, 155-6.
5. Walker, Pg 154-6.
6. See above note.
7. Walker, Pg 156.
8. Walker, Pg 156-7.

Agathodaimon

1. Landfester, Manfred - Cancik, Hubert - Schneider, Helmuth – *Brill's New Pauly Encyclopaedia of the Ancient World,* Pg 189 & Bailey, Donald M. – *A Snake-Legged Dionysus from Egypt, & Other Divine Snakes,* Pg 266.
2. *Isis-Thermuthis* are Greek versions of the Egyptian goddess, Renenutet. Bailey, Pg 266.
   Known in today as the reef knot, it was used in healing. Wounds bound by it were believed to heal faster. Bailey, 266.
3. Feliciano, João Pedro – *The Agathos Daimon in Greco-Egyptian Religion,* Pg 1.
4. Feliciano, Pg 1-15 & Kuehn, Pg 173.
5. Heptagram – The seven sacred vowels are the Greek *aeêiouô,* associated with the seven planets. The directions were specific. Speaking to the rising sun, the letters were to be pronounced clearly. *A* was spoken while holding the arms to the left, *E* with right fist forward, turning west and stretching out both hands intone Ê. *I* was spoken to the South with both hands on the stomach, after which *O* was spoken in a forward bend, facing the earth and touching the ends of the toes with the hands. Rising to look up at the heavens, and placing the hand to heart, *U* was uttered and finally, still looking to the sky, placing the hands upon the head, came Ô. Feliciano, Pg 9-10.
6. Feliciano, Pg 9.
7. Feliciano, Pg 11.
8. Feliciano, Pg 3, 12.

Abraxas

1. Fideler, David – *Jesus Christ the Sun of God,* Pg 28.
2. Fideler, Pg 28 (365) – Coulter, Charles Russell & Turner, Patricia, Pg 8.
3. Fideler, Pg 28, 256.

IAO is comprised of the Greek vowels: *iota, alpha* and *omega,* and was used in the ceremonies of the gnostics. It also appears in the *Pistis Sophia* when the resurrected Christ shouts out the name thrice. These were the sacred vowels, each pregnant with its own symbolism and power – Fideler, Pg 256.

Chapter 5: What the Dragons Know

1. Campbell, Joseph – *The Masks of God,* Vol III, Pg 26 & Ophis version: Fontenrose, Joseph – Python.
2. Sargent, Denny – *Naga-Magick,* Pg 21.
3. See above; also, Cirlot, J.E – *Dictionary of Symbols,* Pg 47-8, 380.
4. Roob, Alexander – *Alchemy & Mysticism,* Pg 332-5.

Ningishzida – Prince of Dragons

1. Frayne, Douglas R. – *Old Babylonian Period, 2033-1595 BC,* Pg 284 (Chair-bearer) – Black, Jeremy & Green, Anthony – *An Illustrated dictionary of Gods, Demons & Symbols of Ancient Mesopotamia,* Pg 72, 86, (Dumuzi), Black, Jeremy/ Cunningham, Graham/ Robson, Eleanor & Zólyomi, Gábor – *The Literature of Ancient Sumer,* Pg 250 (snakes & Dragons), Price, Ira Maurice – *Great Cylinder Inscription of Gudea,* Pg XV (Enninu).
2. Black, Green et al, Pg 167-8 (Gudea vase, Baśmu), Langdon, S. – *Tammuz and Ishtar,* Pg 7-8 (Tree), Pg 122 (Caduceus).
3. Frothingham, A.L – *The Babylonian Origins of Hermes & the Caduceus,* Pg 182, 184, 185 (Right-hand and Snakes). Langdon, S. – *Tammuz and Ishtar,* Pg 116 (Hydra).
4. Vanderburgh, Frederick Augustus – *Sumerian Hymns,* Pg 72-4, Penglase, Charles – *Greek Myths & Mesopotamia: Parallels & Influence in the Homeric Hymns & Hesiod.* Pg 13-42.
5. Frothingham, Pg 182.
6. Black, Jeremy & Green, Anthony, Pg 27.
7. Frothingham, Pg 191 (sexual ambiguity), Langdon, Pg 4-5.

The Grecian Caduceus

1. Maia, Hermes mother, has gathered numerous myths and tales. Her origins as an earth spirit are obscure – to some she was a nymph who lived in a deep cave on Mount Cyllene. She is also involved in astrological tales that were used to explain the movement of constellations and is said to be the eldest of the Pleiades, daughters of Atlas and Pleïone.
2. This concept is discussed in Lachman, Gary – *The Quest for Hermes Trismegistus* & Frothingham, A.L – *The Babylonian Origins of Hermes & the Caduceus*.
3. Lachman, Gary – *The Quest for Hermes Trismegistus*.
4. See both Lachman & Frothingham. Hermes was also the father of Pan from his union with Penelope Another opposite is concealed here: for Hermes is an ordering principle of mediation, constraint and politic, while Pan is a chaotic wilderness spirit.
5. Frothingham, full article.
   Brisson, Luc – *How Philosophers Saved Myths*, Pg 78.
6. See Boylan, Patrick – *Thoth the Hermes of Egypt*.
7. This information was gleaned from the following texts: Boylan, Patrick – *Thoth the Hermes of Egypt*. Budge, J Wallis – *Gods Of Egypt*. Budge, J Wallis – *The Book of the Dead Papyrus of Ani*. Sauneron, Serge – *The Priests of Ancient Egypt*. Watterson, Barbara – *Gods of Ancient Egypt*.

The Sceptre of the Dragon-King

1. Ward, William Hayes – *Bel & the Dragon*, Pg 96.
2. Lachman, Gary – *The Quest for Hermes Trismegistus*, Pg 12-3.
3. Lachman, Pg 82.
4. MacCulloch, J.A & Moore, George F. – *Myths of All Races*, Vol 5, Pg 53.
5. Lachman, Pg 208-10.
6. *Sender: Prolegomena* – Harrison, Jane Ellen, Pg 26. Rhabdos: Pg 44-5.

7. Sara Kuehn – *The Dragon in Medieval East Christian & Islamic Art*, Pg 186. In Islamic art the imagery of the double dragon, sometimes entwined, knotted or surrounding a figure/face is protective in function. The knotting, weaving is a binding/strengthening of the image's potency. See, Mikayelyan, L. Sh.
8. Frothingham, Pg 205-7.
9. Roob, Alexander – *Alchemy & Mysticism*, Pg 334-7.
10. Christians adopted the symbol for their own ends too.

Chapter 6: What Came First, the Serpent or the Egg?

Dissecting the Dragon

1. It's been postulated that, in China, the totems of various tribes could have formed the parts of the dragon. At some point these tribes had been united under a common banner, they could have lent aspects of their totem to create a hybrid creature. However, such notions lack proof. While being interesting, such 'practical' solutions tend to reduce a complex symbol and phenomena – Zhao, Qiguang – *The Study of Dragons in the East & West.*
2. Zhao discusses this in his book, Pg 2, 15 are relevant here.
3. Sara Kuehn – *The Dragon in Medieval East Christian & Islamic Art*, Pg 7, 11, 88.
4. Mooney, James – *Myths Of The Cherokee*, Pg 481.
5. Mooney, James – *Myths Of The Cherokee*, Pg 296-7, Spence, Lewis – *Myths of the American Indians*, Pg 110 & Crawford, Suzanne J. & Kelley Dennis F. – *American Indian Religious Traditions: an Encyclopaedia*, Pg 675.
6. Spence, Lewis – *Myths of the American Indians*, Pg 274-5.
7. Bingham, Anna – *South and American Mythology A-Z*, Pg 24.
8. Campbell, Joseph – *The Masks of God, Vol I*, Pg 458.
9. Bingham, Pg 94-5.
10. Charing, Howard G. – *Communion With the Infinite.*

11. Lawrie, Margaret Elizabeth – *Myths of the Torres Straits,* Pg 139-42.
12. Lawrie, Pg 370-2.
13. Lynch, Patricia Ann – *African mythology A-Z,* Pg 101.
14. These references are sourced from Lynch and also, Sproul, Barbara C. – *Primal Myths From Around The World.*
15. She discusses this at length with pictorial examples in, Gimbutas, Marija – *The Gods & Goddesses of Old Europe.*
16. Eliade, Mircea – *Shamanism,* Pg 48, 68, 131-3, 152.
17. See Narby, Jeremy – *The Cosmic Serpent,* in which this theme is explored in great detail.
18. Zhao, Pg 148-9.
19. See, Sheldrake, Rupert – *The Presence of the Past: Morphic Resonance & the Memory of Nature.*
20. Clark, R.T Rundle – *Myth & Symbol in Ancient Egypt,* Pg 54.
21. This echoes the Bull-like sky god, such as Marduk. The missing head reminds me of the Goddess figures from Malta, dated between 3000-2500 BCE. These also lack heads, intentionally it appears and no actual heads have been found. It could be that something more perishable was placed upon these large figures. But what does it signify? Could it hint that the Goddess was viewed as somehow *less* than the Bullheaded god? Could it be that our misogyny is innate? I leave this question open. We need to take this in, with all its implications.
22. Biehl, Peter F./Bertemes, François/ Meller, Harald (Editors) – *The Archaeology of Cult and Religion,* Pg 133-8.

Bibliography

Abbott, G.F. – *Macedonian Folklore* (Cambridge University Press, 1903)

Allen, Judy, Griffiths, Jeanne – *The Book of the Dragon* (Chartwell Books, 1979)

Ananikiam, Mardios H. – *Armenian Mythology* (The Mythology of All Races, Vol VII, Cooper Square, 1964)

Asatrian, Garnik – 'Armenian Demonology: A Critical Overview' (Article from, *Iran & The Caucasus*, issue 17, Pg 9-25, 2013)

Aung, Dr. Htin – *Folk Elements in Burmese Buddhism* (U Hla Maung, 1959)

Avenstrup, Áge & Treitel, Elisabeth (trans. Turbes, J.) – *Icelandic Fairy & Folktales* (Legacy Information Services, 2017)

Bailey, Donald M. – 'A Snake-Legged Dionysus from Egypt, & Other Divine Snakes' (*Journal of Egyptian Archaeology*, Vol 93, Pg 263-270 – Egypt Exploration Society, 2007).

Barnabé, Alberto & san Cristóbal, Ana Isabel Jiménez – *Instructions for the Netherworld: the Orphic Gold Tablets* (Brill, 2007)

Barton, George A. – *Tiamat* (Harvard University Press, 1890)

Baudiš, Josef – *Czech Folktales* (Allen & Unwin, 1917)

Bauscatz, Paul – *The Well & The Tree: World & Time in Early Germanic Culture* (The University of Massachusetts Press, 1982)

Biehl, Peter F./Bertemes, François/ Meller, Harald (Editors) – *The Archaeology of Cult and Religion* (Archaeolingua, 2001)

Binchy, D.A. – *The Saga of Fergus mac Léti* (Ériu Vol 16, 1952)

Bingham, Anna – *South and American Mythology A-Z* (Facts on File, 2004)

Black, Jeremy/Cunningham, Graham/ Robson, Eleanor & Zólyomi, Gábor – *The Literature of Ancient Sumer* (Oxford University Press, 2004)

Black, Jeremy & Green, Anthony – *An Illustrated dictionary of Gods, Demons & Symbols of Ancient Mesopotamia* (British Museum Press, 1992)

Bloom, Harold – *Beowulf* (Bloom's Guides, 2008)

Bolger, Diane & Serwint, Nancy (Editors) – 'Engendering Aphrodite: Women & Society in Ancient Cyprus' (*ASOR Archaeological Reports*, Vol 7, 2002)

Bonwick, James – *The Serpent Faith in Ireland* (Samhain Song Press, 2017)

Borghouts, J.F. (Translated by) – *Ancient Egyptian Magical Texts* – E.J Brill, 1978)

Bostock, John & Riley, H.T. – *The Natural History: Pliny the Elder* (Taylor and Francis, 1855)

Boylan, Patrick – *Thoth the Hermes of Egypt* (Oxford University Press, 1922)

Bremmer, Jan & Erskine Andrew – *The gods of ancient Greece: Identities & Transformations* (Edinburgh University Press, 2013)

Bridgman, Timothy P. – *Hyperboreans: Myth & History in Celtic-Hellenic Contacts* (Routledge, 2005)

Brisson, Luc – *How Philosophers Saved Myths: Allegorical Interpretation & Classical Mythology* (University of Chicago Press, 2004)

Brooksbank, F.H. – *Legends of Ancient Egypt* (T.Y. Crowell, 1922)

Brunet, Stephen & Smith R. Scott – *Anthology of Classical Myth* (Hackett Publishing Co., 2004)

Budge, J Wallis – *The Book of the Dead Papyrus of Ani* (The Medici Society, 1913)

Budge, J Wallis – *Gods Of Egypt* (Methuen & Co., 1904)

Budge, E.A Wallis – *Osiris & the Egyptian Resurrection, Vol 1* (Philip Lee Warner, 1911)

Burkert, Walter – *The Orientalizing Revolution Near-Eastern Influence on Greek Culture in Archaic Age* (Harvard University Press, 1998)

Byock, Jesse L. – *The Saga of the Volsungs* (University of California Press, 1990)

Caldwell, Richard – *The Origin of the Gods* (Oxford University Press, 1998)

Campbell, John Francis –*The Celtic Dragon Myth* (J. Grant, 1911)

Campbell, John Francis – *Popular Tales of Western Scotland: Vol 1 - III* (Edmonston & Douglas, 1860)

Campbell, Joseph – *The Masks of God, Vol I* (Secker & Warburg, 1959)

Campbell, Joseph – *The Masks of God - Vol II* (Secker & Warburg, 1959)

Campbell, Joseph – *The Masks of God, Vol III* (Secker & Warburg, 1959)

Cirlot, J.E – *Dictionary of Symbols* (Routledge, 1971)

Chandler, Kenneth – 'Origins of Vedic Civilisation' https://www.academia.edu/27298615/Origins_of_Vedic_Civilization

Charing, Howard G. – 'Communion With the Infinite: The Visual Music of the Shipibo people of the Amazon' (https://www.arte-amazonia.com/shamanism/communion-with-the-infinite-the-visual-music-of-the-shipibo/)

Clark, R.T Rundle – *Myth & Symbol in Ancient Egypt* (Thames & Hudson, 1959)

Collins, Anthony – Karahan – 'Tepe: Its Three Interconnected, Rock-cut Structures Examined' (Paper on, https://www.academia.edu/107393911/Karahan_Tepe_Its_Three_Interconnected_Rock_cut_Structures_Examined)

Cooper, William R. – *Serpent Myths of Ancient Europe* (Robert Hardwicke, 1873)

Corlett, Christiaan – 'The Prehistoric Ritual Landscape of Croagh Patrick, Co. Mayo' – (*Journal of Irish Archaeology*, IX, 1998)

Cornford, F.M – *Principium Sapientiae: The Origins of Greek Philosophical Thought* (Harper & Row, 1965)

Cotterell, Arthur – *Encyclopaedia of Mythology* (Hermes House, 2006)

Coulter, Charles Russell & Turner, Patricia – *Encyclopaedia of Ancient Deities* (Routledge, 2000)

Crawford, Suzanne J. & Kelley Dennis F. – *American Indian Religious Traditions: an Encyclopaedia - Vol 1 A–I* (ABC Clio, 2005)

Curran, John – *Pagan City & Christian Capital* (Clarendon Press, 2000)

Cutillo, Brian & Rinpoche, *Lama Kunga – Drinking the Mountain Stream: Songs of Tibet's Beloved Saint, Milarepa* (Wisdom Publications, 2001)

Dalley, Stephanie – *Myths From Mesopotamia* (Oxford University Press, 1989)

Davidson, H. R. Ellis – *Gods and Myths of Ancient Europe* (Penguin Books, 1964/1990)

Davidson, H R Ellis – *The Lost Beliefs of Northern Europe* (Routledge, 1993)

Day, John – *Yahweh and the Gods and Goddesses of Caanan* (Sheffield Academic Press, 2000)

Debroy, Bibek (Translated by) – *Mahabharata, Vol I* (Penguin Books, 2010)

Dempsey, T. – *The Delphic Oracle: Its Early History, Influence & Fall* (B.H Blackwell, 1918)

Dixon-Kennedy, Mike – *Encyclopaedia of Slavic & Russian Myth & Legend* (ABC Clio, 1998)

Doniger, Wendy (Translated by) – *The Rig Veda* (Penguin 1981)

Dowden, Ken – *European Paganism* (Routledge, 2000)

Dumezil, Georges –*Mitra-Varuna: An Essay on Two Indo-European Representations of Sovereignty* (Zone Books, 1988)

Edwards, Cyril – *Nibelungenlied* (Oxford University Press, 2010)

Edwards, Ruth B. – *Kadmos the Phoenician: a Study in Greek Legends & the Mycenaean Age* (Adolph M. Hakkert, 1979)

Eggeling, Julius (translated by) – *Satapatha-Brâhmana* (Claredon Press, 1882)

Eliade, Mircea – *Patterns in Comparative Religion* (Sheed & Ward, 1958)

Eliade, Mircea – *Shamanism: Archaic Techniques of Ecstasy* (Princeton University Press, 1974)

Eliade, Mircea – *Yoga* (Routledge, 1958)

Esmerović, Raif – *Cult of the Snake in Bosnia* (unknown)

Feliciano, João Pedro – 'The Agathos Daimon in Greco-Egyptian Religion' (Article at, https://www.academia.edu/27115429/The_Agathos_Daimon_in_Greco_Egyptian_religion,

Fergusson, James – *Tree & Serpent Worship* (W.H Allen & Co., 1868)

Fideler, David – *Jesus Christ the Sun of God: Ancient Cosmology & Early Christian Symbolism* (Quest Books, 1993)

Fisher, John & Gould, S. Baring – *Lives of the British Saints* (C.J. Clark, 1907)

Folkard Jnr, Richard – *Plant Lore Legends & Lyrics* (Sampson Low, Martson & Co, 1892)

Fontenrose, Joseph – *Python: A study of the Delphic Myth and its origins* (University of California Press, 1959/1980 edition)

Foulke, William Dudley – *History of the Lombards: Paul the Deacon* (Dept, History, University of Pennsylvania, 1907)

Frazer, James – *The Golden Bough* (Macmillan & Co, 1923)

Frayne, Douglas R. – *Old Babylonian Period, 2033-1595 BC* (University of Toronto Press, 1990)

Frothingham, A.L – 'The Babylonian Origins of Hermes & the Caduceus I' (Article from, *American Journal of Archaeology*, Vol 20, Pg 175-211, 1916)

Frothingham, A.L – 'Medusa, Apollo & the Great Mother' (Article from *American journal of Archaeology*, Vol 15, 1911)

Gimbutas, Marija – *The Gods & Goddesses of Old Europe* (University of California Press, 1984)

Goldsmith, Elizabeth E. – *Life Symbols: as Related to Sex Symbolism* (G.P Putnam's Sons, 1924)

Grabbe, Lester L. – *Ancient Israel* (T&T Clark, 2007)

Grant, Michael & Hazel, John – *Who's Who In Classical Mythology* (Routledge 2002)

Green, Miranda Alehouse – *Bog Bodies Uncovered* (Thames & Hudson, 2015)

Green, Miranda – *Symbol & Image In Celtic Religious Art* (Routledge, 1989)

Grimal, Pierre – *A Concise Dictionary of Classical Mythology* (Basil Blackwell, 1990)

Gwynn, Edward – *The Metrical Dindshenchas, Part IV* (Royal Irish Academy Vol X, The Todd Lectures Series, Hodges, Figgis & Co., 1924)

Hale, Wash Edward – *Asura in Early Vedic Religion* (Motilal Banarsidass, 1986)

Hall, James – *Illustrated Dictionary of Symbols* (John Murray, 1994)

Hardinge, Leslie – *The Celtic Church in Britain* (Church historical Society 1972)

Harrison, Jane Ellen – *Prolegomena* (Cambridge University Press, 1908)

Harrison, Jane Ellen – *Themis; a study of the social origins of Greek Religion,* (Cambridge University Press, 1912)

Hedeager, Lotte – *Iron Age myth & Materiality* (Routledge, 2011)

Hinnells, John R – *Persian Mythology* (Chancellor Press, 1997)

Hooke, S. H. – *Babylonian Art* (Hutchinson's University Library,1953)

Hunt, Norman Bancroft – *Living in Ancient Mesopotamia* (Facts on File, 2010)

Jackson, Jake – *Native American Myths* (Flame Tree Books 2014)

Jean, Georges – *Signs Symbols & Ciphers* (Thames & Hudson, 1999)

Jesch, Judith – *Ships & Men in the Late Viking Age: the Vocabulary of Runic Inscriptions & Skaldic Verse* (Boydell & Brewer, 2001)

Jones, M.A & Ormerod, Henry A – *Pausanias: A Description of Greece* (William Heinemann, 1918)

Jones, T. Gwynn – *Welsh Folklore & Folk-Custom* (Brewer, 1979)

Jung, Carl K. – *Man & His Symbols* (Dell Publishing, 1997)

Kenoyer, Jonathan Mark – 'Indus Seals: an Overview of Iconography & Style' – (*Ancient Sindh, Annual Journal of Research* Vol 9, 2006-2007)

Kenoyer, Jonathan Mark – *Measuring the Harappan World* (Archaeology of Measurement: Ed Iain Morley, 2010)

Kramer, Samuel Noah – *Sumerians: Their History, Culture & Character* (University of Chicago Press, 1971)

Kuehn, Sara – *The Dragon in Medieval East Christian & Islamic Art* (Brill, 2011)

Kuiper, Kathleen – *Mesopotamia: the World's Earliest Civilisation* (Rosen Education Service, 2010)

Kunz, George Frederick – *The Curious Lore of Precious Stones* (J.B. Lippincott, 1913)

Lachman, Gary – *The Quest for Hermes Trismegistus* (Floris Books, 2011)

Landfester, Manfred - Cancik, Hubert - Schneider, Helmuth – *Brill's New Pauly Encyclopaedia of the Ancient World: Vol 1* (Brill, 2006)

Langdon, Stephen – *Sumerian Liturgical Texts* (Philadelphia University Museum, 1917)

Langdon, Stephen – *Tammuz and Ishtar* (Clarendon Press, 1914)

Lawrie, Margaret Elizabeth – *Myths of the Torres Straits* (University of Queensland Press, 1970)

Lecouteux, Claude – *An Encyclopaedia of Norse & Germanic Folklore, Mythology & Magic* (Inner Traditions Bear & Co, 2016)

Lecouteux, Claude – *Demons & Spirits of the Land: Ancestral Lore & Practices* (Inner Traditions, 2015)

Lichtheim, Miriam – *Ancient Egyptian Literature, Vol 1: The Old & Middle Kingdoms* (University of California Press, 2006)

Lies, Betty Bonham – *Earth's Daughters: Stories of Women in Classical Mythology* (Fulcrum Publishing, 1999)

Lindow, John – *Norse Mythology: A Guide to the Gods, Heroes, Rituals and Beliefs* (Oxford University Press, 2001)

Long, Roger – *Curious Oxfordshire* (Sutton Publishing 2008)

Lucas, Mrs. Edgar (Translated by) – *Fairy Tales of the Brother Grimm* (Doubleday, Page & Co, 1909)

Lugira, Aloysius M. – *African Traditional Religion* (Chelsea House Publishers, 2009)

Lyle, Emily (Editor) – *Celtic Myth in the 21st Century: the Gods & Their Stories in a Global Perspective* (University of Wales Press, 2018)

Lynch, Patricia Ann – *African mythology A-Z* (Facts on File, 2004)

MacCulloch, J.A & Moore, George F. – *Myths of All Races, Vol 5* (Plimpton Press, 1931)

MacKenzie, Donald A. – *Myths of Babylonia and Assyria* (The Gresham Publishing Co., 1937)

MacKinlay, James M. – *Folklore of Scottish Lochs & Springs* (William Hodge & Co., 1893)

MacLeod, Sharon Paice –*Celtic Myth & Religion: A Study of Traditional Belief With Newly Translated Prayers, Poems & Songs* (Jefferson, 2012)

MacNeill Eoin – *Duanaire Finn: The Book of the Lays of Fionn, Vol 1* (Irish Texts Society, 1908)

MacQueen, J.C – *Hittites & Their Contemporaries in Asia Minor* (Thames & Hudson, 1996)

McHardy, Stuart – *The Quest for the Nine Maidens* (Luath Press, 2003)

McIntosh, Jane R. – *The Ancient Indus Valleys: A New Perspective* (ABC Clio, 2008)

Malandra, William W. – *An Introduction to Ancient Iranian Religion* (University of Minnesota Press, 1983)

March, Jennifer R. – *Cassell's Dictionary of Classical Mythology* (Cassell & Co., 2001)

Matasovič, Ranko – *A Reader in Comparative Indo-European Religion* (University of Zagreb, 2010)

Milošević , Nikola – *Old Slavic Gods* (https://www.scribd.com/document/293753801/Old-Slavic-Gods)

Mead, George Robert Stow – *Pistis Sophia* (Theosophical Publishing Society, 1896)

Mikayelyan, L. Sh – *Various Aspects of the Image of a Dragon-serpent in Armenian & South Caucasian Sculpture* (Science Committee of the Ministry of Education, Culture & Sports, 2019)

Monaghan, Patricia – *Encyclopaedia of Celtic Mythology & Folklore* (Facts on File. Inc, 2004)

Mookerjee, Ajit – *Kundalini: the Arousal of Inner Energy* (Thames & Hudson, 1982)

Mooney, James – *Myths Of The Cherokee* (Washington Government Printing Office, 1902)

Moore, George F. & Gray, Lewis H. – *Mythology of all Races, Volume VI* (Marshall Jones Co. 1917)

Muller, Max (Translated by) – *Khândogya-Upanishad* (Dover Publications, 2012)

Mumford, John – *Ecstasy Through Tantra* (Llewellyn Publications, 2002)

Mundkur, Balaji – *The Cult of the Serpent* (State University of New York Press, 1983)

Narby, Jeremy – *The Cosmic Serpent* (Weidenfeld & Nicholson, 1999)

Nardo, Don – *The Greenhaven Encyclopaedia of Ancient Mesopotamia* (Greenhaven Press, 2007)

Newman, Paul – *The Hill of the Dragon: An Enquiry into the Nature of Dragon Legends* (Kingsmead Press, 1979)

O'Connor, Daniel – *St Patrick's Purgatory, Lough Derg* (J. Duffy, 1895)

O'Grady, Standish Hayes – *The Pursuit of Dairmuid and Grainne* (Society for the preservation of the Irish Language, M.H. Gill & Son, 1887)

Oldfather, C.D (Translated by) – 'Library of History: Diodorus of Sicily' (University of Chicago Website, https://archive.org/details/DiodorosOfSicily034.598/Diodoros%20of%20Sicily%2001%20%281.1-2.34%29/

Parpola, Asko – *The Roots of Hinduism* (Oxford University Press)

Pavitt, Kate & Thomas, William – *Book of Talismans: Amulets & Zodiacal Gems* (Rider, 1922)

Peck, Harry Thurston – *Harpers Dictionary of Classical Antiquities* (Harper & Bros, 1896)

Penglase, Charles – *Greek Myths & Mesopotamia: Parallels & Influence in the Homeric Hymns & Hesiod* (Routledge 1994)

Pennick, Nigel – *The Celtic Cross: an Illustrated History & Celebration* (Cassell Illustrated, 1998)

Penny, George – *Traditions of Perth* (HardPress Ltd, 2019)

Petropoulos, J. C. B – *Greek Magic* (Routledge, 2008)

Piggott, Juliett – *Japanese Mythology* (Hamlyn Publishing Group, 1973)

Pregadio, Fabrizio – *The Way of the Golden Elixir: An Introduction to Taoist Alchemy* (Golden elixir Press, 2019)

Price, Ira Maurice – *Great Cylinder Inscription of Gudea* (J. C Hinrichs'sche Buchhandlung, 1899)

Queffelec, Henri – *Insight Guide, Brittany* (First Edition, APA Publications Ltd, 1994)

Queffelec, Henri – *Un Recteur De L'ile De Sein* (George G. Harrap & Co. Ltd., 1972)

Radau, Hugo – *The Creation Story of Genesis I and Sumerian Theogony & Cosmology* (Open Court Publishing Co., 1902)

Raina, Mohini Qasba – *Kasur the Kashmiri Speaking People: Analytical Perspective* (Partridge Singapore, 2014)

Rees, Alwyn & Brinley – *Celtic Heritage: Ancient Tradition in Ireland & Wales* (Thames & Hudson, 1961)

Reemes, Dana Michael – *The Egyptian Ouroboros* (University of California, 2015)

Remler, Pat – *Egyptian Mythology A-Z* (Chelsea House Publishers, 2010)

Richardson, John – *The Great Folly, Superstition, & Idolatry of Pilgrimages in Ireland; especially of that to St. Patrick's purgatory.*

Together with an account of the loss that the public sustaineth thereby; truly and impartially represented – (J. Hyde, 1727)

Rillo, Arturo G. – *The Greek Origin of the Caduceum: Æsculapius* – (Columbia Médica, Vol 39, no.4, Pg 389-93, 2008)

Roob, Alexander – *Alchemy & Mysticism* (Taschen, 2015)

Room, Adrian – *Who's Who In Classical Mythology* (Gramercy Books, 2003)

Ross, Anne – *Druids: Preachers of Immortality* (Tempus, 1999)

Ross, J. – *The Book of Scottish Poems, Ancient & Modern* (The Edinburgh Publishing Company 1878)

Ross, Margaret Clunies – *A History of Old Norse Poetry & Poetics* (Boydell & Brewer Ltd, 2005)

Sargent, Denny – *Naga-Magick: The Wisdom of the Serpent Lords* (The Original Falcon Press, 2014)

Saunders, N.K. – *The Epic of Gilgamesh* (Assyrian News Agency

Sauneron, Serge – *The Priests of Ancient Egypt* (Evergreen Books, 1960)

Scott, Michael – *Delphi: A History of the Centre of the Ancient World* (Princeton University Press, 2015)

Sheppard, H. J. – 'The Ouroboros & the Unity of Matter in Alchemy' (From *Ambix*, Vol 10, Issue 2, Pg 83-96, 1962)

Sheldrake, Rupert – *The Presence of the Past: Morphic Resonance & the Memory of Nature* (Park St Press, 2012)

Seymour, St. John D. – *St Patrick's Purgatory: A Medieval Pilgrimage in Ireland* (W. Tempest, 1918)

Silberer, Herbert – *The Hidden Symbolism of Alchemy* (Dover Publications Inc., 1971)

Simpson, Jacqueline – *European Mythology* (P. Bedrick Books, 1987)

Smith, James Reuel – *Springs & Wells in Greek & Roman Literature: Their Legends & Locations* (G.P. Putnam's Sons, 1922)

Smith, Mark S. – *The Ugaritic Baal Cycle* (Brill, 1994)

Spence, Lewis – *Legends & Romances of Brittany* (Frederick A. Stokes 1917)

Spence, Lewis – *Myths of the American Indians* (George G. Harrap & Son, 1916)

Spence, Lewis – *Myths of Babylonia and Assyria* (G. Harrap, 1916)

Sproul, Barbara C. – *Primal Myths From Around The World* (Harper One, 1979)

Stapleton, Michael – *Illustrated Dictionary of Greek & Roman Mythology* (Peter Bedrick Books, 1986)

Takayoshi Oshima – 'The Babylonian God Marduk' (*The Babylonian World,* Edited by Gwendolyn Leick - Ch 24, Pg 348-60, Routledge, 2007)

Tembouret, Kévin – *French Folklore* (Everand)

Temperley, Alan – *Tales of Galloway* – (Skilton & Shaw, 1979)

Todd, Margo – *The Perth Kirk Session Book, 1577-1590* (Scottish history Society 2012)

Uždavinys, Algis – *The Golden Chain: an Anthology of Pythagorean & Platonic Philosophy* (World Wisdom, 2004)

Uždavinys, Algis – *Orpheus and the roots of Platonism* (The Matheson Trust, 2011)

Vanderburgh, Frederick Augustus – *Sumerian Hymns* (The Columba University Press, 1908)

Veelenturf, Kees – 'Visions of the End & Irish High Crosses' (in *Apocalyptic and Eschatological Heritage: The Middle East and Celtic Realms,* Dublin, Portland, 2003, Pg 144-173)

Verrall, Margaret de G. – *Mythology & Monuments of Ancient Ath*ens (Macmillan & Co., 1890)

Vigfusson, Gudbrand & Powell, F. York – *Corpus Poeticcum Boreale* (Claredon Press, 1883)

Vinycomb, John – *Fictitious & Symbolic Creatures in Art: With Specific Reference to Their Use in British Heraldry* (Ballantyne & Co., 1906)

Vogel, Joseph – *Indian Serpent Lore: Nâgas in Hindu Legend & Art* (Arthur Probstain, 1926)

Walker, Benjamin – *Gnosticism, its History & Influence* (The Aquarian Press, 1983)

Ward, William Hayes – 'Bel & the Dragon' (*The American Journal of Languages & Literature,* 1898)

Watterson, Barbara – *Gods of Ancient Egypt* (Facts on File Publications, 1984)

West, M.L. – *Indo-European Poetry & Myth* (Oxford University Press, 2007)

West, M. L. – *The Orphic Poems* (Clarendon Press, 1983)

White, Gordon – *Star Ships* (Scarlet Imprint, 2016)

Wilk, Stephen R. – *Medusa: Solving the mystery of the Gorgon* (Oxford University Press, 2000)

Wilkes, John – *The Illyrians* (Blackwell Publishers, 1995)

Wilkinson, Richard H. – *The Complete Gods & Goddesses Of Ancient Europe* (Thames & Hudson, 2017)

Williams, George M. – *Hindu Mythology* (ABC Clio, 2003)

Winterborne, Anthony – *When the Norns Have Spoken* (Fairleigh Dickenson University Press, 2004)

Wyatt, N. – *Religious Texts From Ugarit* (Sheffield Academic Press, 2006)

Zimmer, Heinrich – *Myths & Symbols in Indian Art & Civilisation* (Pantheon Books inc. 1946)

Zhao, Qiguang – *The Study of Dragons in the East & West* (Peter Lang Publishing, 1992)

Other Anon Sources

(Airchaeology.org)

www.duchas.ie

Epicurus Fragment (from Epiphanius) – www.Perseus.com

https://www.livius.org/articles/place/babylon/etemenanki/

Nomination Dossier for Inscription of the Property on the World Heritage List January 2018 (Ministry of Tourism, Republic of Iraq, 2018)

Slayer's Slab – https://www.atlasobscura.com/places/slayers-slab

Surrey Archaeology Bulletin 483 (https://www.surreyarchaeology.org.uk/bulletins)

From the Author

Thanks for purchasing a copy of *Dragons of the Deep*. I hope that it has fuelled your imagination and given you a deeper appreciation for the mythology of the dragon. Writing this book was itself a journey that I began some years back, and it's the result of many a happy hour engrossed in research. If you have a chance, it would be sincerely appreciated if you could review the book on your favourite online site. If you'd like to find out more about my work, please check out my website, thestarlitunder.com. For more info. I also maintain a weekly Substack with an ever-increasing backlog of articles, davecstone.substack.com.

Also by Dave Stone

Gods & Goddesses of the Celtic Realms

Explore the hidden realms of the Celts and discover the gods and goddesses who guided their lives. This thoroughly researched book weaves together history, folklore and myth to bring you closer to the ancient Celtic deities. Whether you're an enthusiast or a scholar, this book is your key to unlocking the mysteries of the Celts.

ISBN-13: 979-8859770953

MOON BOOKS

PAGANISM & SHAMANISM

What is Paganism? A religion, a spirituality, an alternative belief system, nature worship? You can find support for all these definitions (and many more) in dictionaries, encyclopaedias, and text books of religion, but subscribe to any one and the truth will evade you. Above all Paganism is a creative pursuit, an encounter with reality, an exploration of meaning and an expression of the soul. Druids, Heathens, Wiccans and others, all contribute their insights and literary riches to the Pagan tradition. Moon Books invites you to begin or to deepen your own encounter, right here, right now.

If you have enjoyed this book, why not tell other readers by posting a review on your preferred book site.

Bestsellers from Moon Books

Keeping Her Keys
An Introduction to Hekate's Modern Witchcraft
Cyndi Brannen
Blending Hekate, witchcraft and personal development together to create a powerful new magickal perspective.
Paperback: 978-1-78904-075-3 ebook 978-1-78904-076-0

Journey to the Dark Goddess
How to Return to Your Soul
Jane Meredith
Discover the powerful secrets of the Dark Goddess and transform your depression, grief and pain into healing and integration.
Paperback: 978-1-84694-677-6 ebook: 978-1-78099-223-5

Shamanic Reiki
Expanded Ways of Working with Universal Life Force Energy
Llyn Roberts, Robert Levy
Shamanism and Reiki are each powerful ways of healing; together, their power multiplies. Shamanic Reiki introduces techniques to help healers and Reiki practitioners tap ancient healing wisdom.
Paperback: 978-1-84694-037-8 ebook: 978-1-84694-650-9

Southern Cunning
Folkloric Witchcraft in the American South
Aaron Oberon
Modern witchcraft with a Southern flair, this book is a journey through the folklore of the American South and a look at the power these stories hold for modern witches.
Paperback: 978-1-78904-196-5 ebook: 978-1-78904-197-2

Bestsellers from Moon Books
Pagan Portals Series

The Morrigan

Meeting the Great Queens

Morgan Daimler

Ancient and enigmatic, the Morrigan reaches out to us. On shadowed wings and in raven's call, meet the ancient Irish goddess of war, battle, prophecy, death, sovereignty, and magic.

Paperback: 978-1-78279-833-0 ebook: 978-1-78279-834-7

The Awen Alone

Walking the Path of the Solitary Druid

Joanna van der Hoeven

An introductory guide for the solitary Druid, The Awen Alone will accompany you as you explore, and seek out your own place within the natural world.

Paperback: 978-1-78279-547-6 ebook: 978-1-78279-546-9

Moon Magic

Rachel Patterson

An introduction to working with the phases of the Moon, what they are and how to live in harmony with the lunar year and to utilise all the magical powers it provides.

Paperback: 978-1-78279-281-9 ebook: 978-1-78279-282-6

Hekate

A Devotional

Vivienne Moss

Hekate, Queen of Witches and the Shadow-Lands, haunts the pages of this devotional bringing magic and enchantment into your lives.

Paperback: 978-1-78535-161-7 ebook: 978-1-78535-162-4